200 QUICK LOOKS
AT FLORIDA HISTORY

James C. Clark

Pineapple Press, Inc.
Sarasota, Florida

To true friends:
Mary Stokes, Beverly Kees, Richard Crepeau, Carl Leubsdorf,
David Colburn, Juliet Zucchelli, and Rob Johnson

Copyright © 2000 by James C. Clark

Photographs courtesy of the Florida State Archives

Inquiries should be addressed to:

Pineapple Press, Inc.
P.O. Box 3889
Sarasota, Florida 34230

www.pineapplepress.com.

Library of Congress Cataloging in Publication Data

Clark, James C., 1947–
    200 quick looks at Florida history/by James C. Clark.
        p.   cm.
    Includes index.
    ISBN 1-56164-200-2 (pbk : alk. paper)
        1. Florida—History—Miscellanea. I. Title: Two hundred quick looks at
        Florida history.
    II. Title.

F311.6.C57 2000
975.9—dc21   00-031360

First Edition
10 9 8 7 6 5 4 3 2

Design by Shé Sicks
Printed in the United States of America

TABLE OF CONTENTS

ACKNOWLEDGMENTS

These articles originally appeared in the *Sun Sentinel* of south Florida and *The Orlando Sentinel* over a ten-year period. During that time, dozens of editors gave their time to make them better. The idea for a column came from former *Orlando Sentinel* editor C. David Burgin. He saw that thousands of new residents were moving into Florida each week and thought they would enjoy a weekly journey through Florida history.

My appreciation of Florida history comes from many people. The long list includes Michael Gannon, Sam Proctor, and David Colburn of the University of Florida; Richard Crepeau and Jerrell Shofner of the University of Central Florida; and Evans Johnson and Kevin O'Keefe of Stetson University.

In addition to the editors at Pineapple Press, I am grateful for the advice of Julian Pleasants of the University of Florida and Gary Mormino of the University of South Florida. As always, Joan Morris of the Florida Archives gave generously of her time.

And of course, nothing would be possible without the support of my sons, Kevin Clark and Randall Clark, and my friend, Mary Stokes.

THE FIRST FLORIDIANS

1 — The First Floridians Arrived More Than Ten Thousand Years Ago

THE FIRST FLORIDIANS ARRIVED IN FLORIDA MORE THAN TEN thousand years ago. Their ancestors traveled across the Bering Strait, and over several hundred years gradually made their way to Florida. They were hunters who wandered throughout Florida.

Florida was a much different place then. It was cooler and home to herds of animals that roamed the area, much like animals on the African plains. There were huge herds of bison and deer.

Florida was larger, with the shoreline much farther into the Atlantic Ocean and the Gulf of Mexico. The end of the last Ice Age raised the water level and pushed the shore miles inland. The Florida climate became warmer, much as it is today.

The changes in the weather brought the vast herds to an end, and the natives had to change their lifestyle. They began hunting smaller animals and foraging for berries and nuts, and they built small camps to be used as bases.

The men hunted and returned to their families at the camp. Often a tribe would have more than one base camp, traveling between several camps as the seasons changed. Nearly four thousand years ago, the Florida natives began to make pottery and to plant and harvest crops.

Tribes formed governments, usually led by chiefs. The chiefs were selected much the same way as European royalty, with titles passed down. One major difference was that although men were chiefs, the line of succession was determined by the female's side of the family.

The largest tribe was the Timucuans of northeast Florida. Within the Timucuans were a dozen different groups, which shared a common language but little else. Even among the various Timucuan groups there were frequent battles over territory.

WHEN PONCE DE LEÓN LANDED NEAR DAYTONA BEACH IN 1513 there were nearly one hundred thousand Indians living in Florida. Almost immediately, the Indians began dying by the thousands, as the Spanish brought new diseases, such as smallpox and syphilis.

Other Indians were killed by Spanish soldiers, some were enslaved, and others fled. When the Spanish surrendered Florida to the British in 1763, they took many of the remaining native Florida Indians with them to Cuba. Then Indians from Georgia and Alabama began moving into Florida, settling near what are now Tallahassee and Gainesville.

The most powerful were the Creeks, who settled in north Florida. The British signed treaties with the Creeks and generally lived in peace. The Creeks were often nomads, and the Spanish named them *cimarrones*, which meant "wild ones" or "runaways." Over time, the word changed to "Seminole."

Soon Seminole villages dotted the territory from Tallahassee to Lake Okeechobee. After the American Revolution, relations between the Americans and the Indians became worse. During the First Seminole War, General Andrew Jackson led an expedition and forced the Seminoles to retreat from north Florida.

A treaty signed in 1823 established a reservation for the Seminoles from Ocala to Lake Okeechobee. The reservation did not last long. Whites pressed to have the Indians removed, and the U.S. government established a reservation for the Indians in Oklahoma.

Many of the Indians refused to move, touching off the Second Seminole War. About fifteen hundred Seminoles used guerrilla tactics to hold back as many as nine thousand American soldiers. It became a war of attrition, and eventually all but three hundred Seminoles were forcibly moved to Oklahoma. The three hundred hid in the Everglades to avoid capture, and today's Seminoles are descended from that very small band.

3 The Legend of Pocahontas Began in Florida, Not Virginia

EVERY SCHOOL CHILD HAS HEARD THE STORY: CAPTAIN JOHN Smith is about to be executed by Indians at Jamestown, Virginia, when Pocahontas steps in and urges her father, the chief, to spare him. It is a wonderful story, but it did not happen in

Jamestown; it happened in Florida.

It all started in 1539 when Hernando de Soto landed at Tampa Bay. The landing party found a man who appeared to be an Indian, but spoke perfect Spanish. He turned out to be Juan Ortíz, a soldier from an earlier Spanish expedition who had been captured by the Indians, enslaved, and tortured.

The chief of the Timucuan tribe wanted to put Ortíz to death and was roasting him alive when the chief's daughter and his wife heard Ortíz crying out. They removed him from the grill, carried him to their hut, and treated him until he was better.

The exploits of Ortíz were written about and seen by a biographer of Captain John Smith. The writer thought it was a wonderful story and used it in a biography about Smith. Smith thought it such a good tale that he told people it was true, even though he had not mentioned it to anyone earlier. Because more people read English history books than Spanish history books, Smith's story was accepted and Ortíz was forgotten.

There is one thing Ortíz will always be remembered for: the creation of an American cuisine. When the Spanish asked Ortíz about his ordeal, he used the Indian word *barbacoa* to describe being roasted. The word changed slightly, although it is still with us: Ortíz said his captors tried to barbecue him.

4 A Trick Led to the Capture of the Indian Chief Osceola

IN 1823 THE UNITED STATES GOVERNMENT SIGNED A TREATY with the Indians of Florida. The Indians received a four-million-acre reservation, cash payments for twenty years, and other aid. Seven years later, the United States changed its policy. Congress passed the Indian Removal Act, calling for the Indians to be moved from Florida to places such as Arkansas and Oklahoma.

When the government asked the Indians to sign the new treaty, Osceola, a young Indian leader, stepped forward and plunged his knife into the document. "The only treaty I will execute is with this!" he said. After that, Osceola and his men played havoc with government troops. A string of generals could not kill or capture the leader, who attacked at will.

Finally, Osceola agreed to meet with General Thomas Jessup under a flag of truce, but Jessup had a trick up his sleeve. When Osceola showed up to talk, Jessup took him into custody. Even though Osceola had been attacking United States troops, Jessup was criticized for arresting Osceola under a flag of truce. The uproar was so great that Congress ordered an investigation, and Jessup spent the rest of his life explaining his actions.

Meanwhile, Osceola was imprisoned with his two wives and his children in St. Augustine. Officials worried there might be an attempt to free him, and he was moved with nearly two hundred other Indians to a prison in Charleston, South Carolina. By the time he got to Charleston he was dying from an inflammation of the tonsils. He dressed in his finest warrior clothes, shook hands with the Indians in his party, folded his hands across his chest, smiled, and died.

Then, in one of the strangest twists of events, Osceola's doctor, Frederick Weedon, cut Osceola's head off and preserved it. It ended up in a medical museum in New York, where it was destroyed by fire in 1866. The rest of his remains are buried in Charleston.

5   Wanting a Fair Deal for the Indians Ended William Harney's Military Career

YOU HAVE HEARD OF DAVY CROCKETT AND JIM BOWIE, THE heroes of the Alamo and Texas independence. Sam Houston's name may be familiar also, but it's a lot less likely that you have ever heard of William Harney. It was Harney whose brilliant military tactics routed the Mexican Army in a decisive battle of the Mexican-American War.

But if Harney is little remembered for his actions in Texas, he is nearly forgotten for his role in Florida. Only Seminole County's Lake Harney and Hillsborough County's Harney Road stand as tributes to his accomplishments.

Harney was not like most soldiers. He opposed battling the Seminoles and urged the government to allow them to remain in south Florida. Harney set up a meeting with the Indian leader Osceola to discuss a treaty. Unknown to Harney, his superiors planned a devious surprise. Instead of negotiating with Osceola, the soldiers took him prisoner and he died in captivity.

The army was criticized for its deception and accepted Harney's original advice to open negotiations with the Indians. Harney was later named commander of the American troops in the West and continued to work for Indian rights. His sympathy for Indian rights angered his fellow officers, so he was passed over for command in the Civil War, a decision Abraham Lincoln later called "one of the greatest mistakes of my administration." Harney retired as a major general and returned to Florida.

6 Tricking Florida's Indians For All They Were Worth

FLORIDA'S MOST EXCLUSIVE CITY, PALM BEACH, SITS ON Lake Worth. The lake was named for Colonel William J. Worth, an Indian fighter whose success rested on lies and trickery. Worth came to Florida around 1840 to continue the long-running war against the Seminoles.

The Indian leader Coacoochee had already surrendered to the troops and was shipped off to the West. Worth thought Coacoochee might be useful in getting the remaining Indians to surrender. Coacoochee was returned to Florida and forced to help Worth. But Coacoochee also criticized the whites for the way they dealt with the Indians:

"[The White Man] said he was my friend; he abused our women and children, and told us to go from the land. Still he gave me his hand in friendship; we took it. . . . He had a snake in the other; his tongue was forked; he lied, and stung us. I asked but for a small piece of these lands, enough to plant and to live upon, far south, a spot where I could place the ashes of my kindred, a spot only sufficient upon which I could lay my wife and child. This was not granted me."

His eloquence did not sway Worth, whose plan worked—320 Indians surrendered and were taken to Oklahoma. They were ill prepared for the Oklahoma winter, lacking proper housing and food, and many died. Back in Florida, Worth tried to get more Indians to surrender and be transported to Oklahoma. He displayed a white flag of truce and lured more than one hundred Indians to their capture.

There were only about three hundred Indians left in south Florida, and they were living on the run in the swamps. Worth simply gave up, declared an end to the war on August 14, 1842, and left Florida. He was promoted to brigadier general for his work.

7 The Mystery Remains: How Did the Indian Chief Escape?

IT IS STILL A MYSTERY AND WILL ALMOST CERTAINLY REMAIN that way. How did Seminole Indian chief Coacoochee and nineteen of his followers escape from the "escape-proof" fortress at St. Augustine? Their escape prolonged the Seminole War, which started when the United States tried to move Florida Indians to Arkansas and Oklahoma.

The arrest of Coacoochee and his fellow tribal leaders seemed to mark the end of the war. Coacoochee was an unusual chief. During one raiding party, he seized a group of Shakespearean actors. Later, at a meeting with General W. J. Worth, he arrived dressed as Hamlet. One of his aides dressed as Richard III.

He was captured in early October 1837 and taken to Fort Marion in St. Augustine. The huge fort, built by the Spanish with five-foot-thick walls, seemed to be the perfect place to hold the chief. The chief and his party were placed in a cell thirty-three feet square, with one door and a small opening to let in light and air about fifteen feet above the floor.

Coacoochee, (Wild Cat)

Seminole Chief Coacoochee

On the outside of the opening, which was eighteen inches by eight inches, there was a twenty-eight-foot drop to the moat below. In addition there were two iron bars blocking the opening. The chief believed he could squeeze through the opening. There is much debate about how the bars were removed. Some believe a file was smuggled into the cell by a sympathizer. Military officials claimed the bars had become corroded and weak.

The prisoners spent several weeks tearing strips from their clothing and turning them into a rope. The Indians were given burlap bags to sleep on, and they also used these to fashion ropes. The Indians, already slender, ate little if any food during their final days of captivity.

They waited until there was no moon, and on the night of November 19, 1837, they made their escape. It was difficult squeezing through the opening and the chief later wrote that "the sharp stones took the skin off my breast and back." Some of the Indians were covered with blood when they finally reached the ground.

Once freed, the chief united Indian opposition to the United States. Still, it was a war of attrition, and gradually the American forces overwhelmed the Indians. In 1841 Coacoochee and three hundred of his followers surrendered and were moved to the West.

8   A Law the Indians Hated Became Their Salvation

IN 1934 CONGRESS PASSED THE WHEELER-HOWARD BILL. IT is better known as the Indian Reorganization Act, although even under that name few have heard of it. It was one of the hundreds of New Deal programs passed during the Roosevelt administration.

Most Indians hated the act, seeing it as more government interference. But it turned out to be very important to the Seminole Indians. The act was to go into effect in 1935, unless tribes voted not to be included.

Throughout the country, most tribal leaders urged Indians to boycott the election. In Florida there were five-hundred eligible Indian voters, but only twenty-one went to the polls. Because all twenty-one voted for the measure, the government considered it approved by the Seminoles.

The act contained provisions for improving health services, education, and tribal self-governance, along with preserving tribal lands. One provision of the act did not seem very important at the time. It exempted the Seminoles from paying state and local taxes.

It was not until 1957 that the Florida Seminoles created their own government under the 1934 act. The Seminoles owned more than two hundred thousand acres in south Florida, but much of it was unproductive. Indians were among the most deprived citizens in Florida.

During much of the 1800s, they subsisted by hunting and fishing in the Everglades and doing some farming. When a project to drain the Everglades began around 1906, the Indians lost a valuable part of their holdings.

In the 1970s, the Florida Seminoles began to take advantage of their exemption from federal and state taxes, selling cut-rate cigarettes at their reservation. The Broward County sheriff filed suit against the Seminoles to stop the tax-free sale of cigarettes, but the federal courts upheld the Indians' right to sell tax-free cigarettes.

In 1979 the Seminoles set up high-stakes bingo games. While state law limited prizes to $250, the Indians were able to offer $10,000 prizes and new cars. The Indians found themselves back in court. And once again the Seminoles won, and they expanded their bingo interests. The 1934 law the Indians did not want turned out to be the economic salvation of their tribe.

EARLY FLORIDA

Where Was the First European Settlement in North America?

A QUIZ: THE FIRST ATTEMPT BY EUROPEANS TO ESTABLISH A town in North America was in
  A. Plymouth, Massachusetts
  B. Roanoke, North Carolina
  C. St. Augustine, Florida
  D. Jamestown, Virginia
  E. None of the above

The answer is none of the above. The first attempt to settle in America was at Pensacola, by an explorer who is nearly forgotten.

Spanish explorer Panfilo de Narváez first sighted what is now the Pensacola area in 1528. Another explorer, Cristóbal Maldonado, spent the winter there in 1539, but failed to get support from the king to establish a settlement. Finally, in 1558, Tristan de Luna established a colony in Pensacola with fifteen hundred residents. From the start, things did not go well. Finally, in 1560, a hurricane nearly destroyed the colony and the effort was abandoned.

Pensacola remained abandoned, except for an occasional Indian tribe, for more than a century. In 1682 the French explorer René de La Salle arrived in what is now New Orleans and claimed the land for the French, naming it Louisiana. La Salle's attempt to settle the Pensacola area failed, but the Spanish worried that another nation would settle there.

The Spanish showed renewed interest in Pensacola. The Spanish king ordered Pensacola occupied in 1694, but it was not until 1698 that the Spanish returned. This time it was a military expedition with 357 men under the command of Andrew d'Arriola.

The expedition had barely arrived when the French showed up in force. From their ships, they fired cannon shots at Pensacola, then withdrew to establish a fort at nearby Mobile. Spain retained Pensacola for two more centuries. Had the Spanish not claimed Pensacola, Florida would have almost certainly fallen to the French, an event that would have changed the course of American history.

10 They Didn't Look Like Much, but Cows Arrived Here with the Spanish

WHEN EXPLORER JUAN PONCE DE LEÓN LANDED IN FLORIDA in 1512 he had a crew of adventurers and seven Andalusian cattle. These animals started the American cattle industry and created what evolved into Texas longhorns.

Before Texas became famous for cows, Florida was one of the leading beef producers. During the Civil War, Florida provided most of the Confederacy's beef and leather. After the Civil War, Florida's cattle industry expanded. The first cows were very different. The size of donkeys, they produced miserable milk and beef, but they could survive in wilderness areas where bigger cows could not.

11 The Spanish Landed Somewhere: The Big Question Is Where

EVERY SCHOOLCHILD KNOWS THAT PONCE DE LEÓN DISCOVered Florida. Other explorers may have been here sooner, and there were already thousands of Indians living in the area, but Ponce got the credit. What is unclear is where he actually landed in 1513.

About ninety years after Ponce landed, the king of Spain asked a man named Herrera to write a history of Spanish exploration. Herrera is believed to have seen Ponce's log (which has since disappeared), and he claimed the explorer landed at thirty degrees, eight minutes north latitude. That would put him just north of St. Augustine.

Plenty of people are dubious about Herrera's conclusions. Navigational sightings were not very reliable then, and Ponce and his crew were off on every sighting by a degree or two. Allowing for error, the most credible spot for a landing was Daytona Beach. Herrera gives exact figures about the depth of the water where Ponce landed, and those figures argue for a landing near Ormond-by-the-Sea.

About the only thing that can be said for sure is that Ponce landed somewhere between Jacksonville and Cape Canaveral. Wherever it was, it was not much of a landing. Ponce came ashore, claimed the land for the king, looked around a bit, and got back on his ship. He then moved down the east coast of Florida, stopping a couple of times around Jupiter Inlet and Miami, and then moving up the west coast, probably to Charlotte Harbor, before returning to Puerto Rico.

12 Being Governor of Florida Was Not Exactly an Honor

FLORIDA'S FIRST GOVERNORS HAD A TOUGH TIME. FROM 1565 to 1763, when Spain ruled Florida, the king appointed governors—not that anyone wanted to be Florida's governor. It was the lowest job in the Spanish empire, because Florida lacked the gold and other riches that would make a governor wealthy.

And there was the matter of pay: The governor of Mexico took home about twenty thousand ducats a year—the governor of Florida just one thousand. If you were named governor of Florida, you could be sure your career in the Spanish government was on the way down. Some even refused the job, running the risk of angering the king. Those who took it were supposed to stay for only five or six years, but some stayed longer because successors delayed coming as long as possible.

The list of early governors was a study in tragedy. The first governor, Pedro Menéndez, died in office, and his successor deserted. Rodrigo de Junco did not even make it to Florida: He drowned while sailing from Spain. His successor was deposed by a mutiny, and the next governor was arrested. The chance of finishing a term as governor of Florida was about one in four.

13 The Early Spanish Envisioned Florida as a Great Empire

WHEN PEDRO MENÉNDEZ ARRIVED TO SETTLE ST. AUGUSTINE in 1565, he had a plan approved by the king of Spain to establish a Spanish empire in North America. The king envisioned a colony stretching from Newfoundland down to what is now South Carolina, then West to the Pacific.

Although Menéndez landed in St. Augustine, he originally planned to establish his headquarters in South Carolina and rule Spain's empire from there. Spanish officials believed that somewhere between Newfoundland and the Chesapeake Bay a river flowed from the Atlantic Ocean to the

Pacific. The river would be a shortcut to the riches of Asia, and Spain would control it.

Of course, Menéndez never found his route to Asia, and his expansion plans were largely limited to Florida. He thought that the St. Johns River flowed down to Lake Okeechobee, then west to the Gulf of Mexico. By following that route, ships would avoid the dangerous keys and make better time. He found out that the St. Johns flowed north.

On his first trip on the St. Johns, Menéndez was forced to stop near the present site of Sanford after Indians put stakes in the river. He set up some settlements along the St. Johns and in south Florida but later abandoned them. As English and French settlers began to arrive, the Spanish empire in North America became smaller and smaller until it included just Florida.

14 Once Huge, Florida Shrank as Everyone Took a Piece

IF THE SPANISH HAD COME OUT ON TOP INSTEAD OF THE British, Florida would look a lot different today. It would be bigger—about the size of Texas—and would include such cities as Charleston, Savannah, Mobile, and Atlanta. But the Spanish lost, and half a dozen states ended up taking bites out of Spanish Florida instead.

When the Spanish discovered Florida in the early sixteenth century, they thought it was just another island. They did not realize that the rest of North America was attached.

But the British began setting up colonies along the East Coast and the Spanish were too weak to defend their claims. The Spanish built garrisons as far north as present-day South Carolina, but the more powerful British established the colony of Carolina and the Spanish were forced to withdraw. Georgia came next, and Florida grew smaller yet. What was left of Florida was still imposing, stretching to the Mississippi River.

A 1763 British map

In 1775 there were

two Floridas: East Florida stretched from the Apalachicola River to the Florida Keys. West Florida extended west to include part of what is today Louisiana and north to include half of what are now Alabama and Mississippi.

In 1810 the United States took part of West Florida from Spain and gave it to Louisiana. The Mississippi Territory took the northern part of West Florida, and much of what was left became Mississippi and Alabama, extending to the Gulf of Mexico.

Still, Georgia was not satisfied. The state claimed a large portion of north Florida. The Spanish and Americans agreed to a joint survey to determine the true border. Florida kept its land, but Georgia kept the issue alive until it was decided by the United States Congress nearly eighty years later.

15   After Nine Tries the Spanish Finally Built a Fort That Lasted

IN 1672 THE KING OF SPAIN WORRIED ABOUT ATTACKS ON the settlement at St. Augustine. Since the British had their eyes on Florida as a possible addition to their colonies, the Spanish built a fort to defend St. Augustine. The fort was named the Castillo de San Marcos, a huge structure made of ground-up sea shells. The Castillo was built after nine earlier forts failed to provide enough protection.

For nearly a century the Spanish controlled the fort then turned it over peacefully to the British. The British controlled Florida for about twenty years, then gave it back to the Spanish. In 1821 the United States acquired Florida, and the American flag was raised over the fort on July 10, 1821.

In acquiring Florida, the United States got two forts named San Marcos, one in St. Augustine and the other in St. Marks. To eliminate confusion, the St. Augustine fort was renamed Fort Marion, in honor of the Revolutionary War hero Francis Marion of South Carolina. The fort served a number of purposes, from hospital to jail.

The fort fell into disrepair so serious that a federal grand jury considered the matter and recommended immediate repairs. Congress agreed to spend twenty thousand dollars, but it was not enough to get the job done. The fort's decline continued.

The moat became a dump for garbage, and cattle grazed the fort grounds. When Florida joined the Confederacy in 1861, rebel soldiers occupied the fort for nearly a year. The fort was never threatened, and the need for troops in other areas forced the South to evacuate it. Union soldiers moved in during 1862.

After the Civil War the fort became a warehouse. For six years it was a prison for Indians captured in wars in the West. It also began to attract tourists, even though it was in sorry shape. The federal government finally appropriated money to fix it up, and by 1910 as many as fifty thousand visitors a year were coming to the fort.

In 1924 President Calvin Coolidge declared the fort a national monument, and eventually the Department of the Interior took control. The original Spanish name was restored, and the Castillo de San Marcos became St. Augustine's most popular attraction, drawing more than seven hundred thousand people each year.

16 Cabeza de Vaca's Walk from Florida to Mexico Created a Golden Myth

ALVAR NÚÑEZ CABEZA DE VACA HAD A FEELING THAT THINGS just were not going right. Maybe if someone had listened, his expedition wouldn't have been decimated and he would not have spent eight years wandering the South.

Cabeza was a member of an expedition exploring the area around Tampa Bay in 1528. The expedition leader wanted to look for the gold he heard existed in north Florida. Cabeza thought it was a bad idea but lost the argument. They marched through the interior of Florida, all the way to an area near present-day Tallahassee.

Conditions were harsh and many in the expedition became ill. Eventually, they decided to return to Tampa Bay. Their only hope was to return by sea, but they had no boats. Using all the material they could obtain, they built five boats. Just about everything went wrong. The five boats became separated, and the crew members on Cabeza's boat began to fall ill and die.

Nearly seven weeks after leaving Florida, Cabeza landed on an island off the coast of what is now Texas. He and his men stayed there for a year, unable to refloat their boat. The Indians proved friendly and gave them shelter and food.

As the second winter arrived, the weather turned unusually harsh and food was in short supply. Cabeza's men began to starve. Only three of the eighty men who landed on the island survived.

Eventually, Cabeza reached the mainland. For several years he roamed throughout Texas. Another group of Indians made him a slave. He waited two years before escaping with two companions. They walked to the Pacific Ocean, then south to Mexico City.

Finally, on July 24, 1536, eight years after they had left Tampa Bay,

Cabeza and his companions arrived in Mexico City. The Spanish assumed Cabeza had died with the rest of the party and were stunned to see him.

In Mexico City there was a huge celebration for Cabeza, and he returned to Spain a hero. Cabeza figured he might turn his fame into a governorship of Florida. Instead, he became Florida's first unsuccessful politician. The post went to Hernando de Soto, and Cabeza responded bitterly.

He became the first European to lie about Florida real estate. He gave people in Spain the impression that there was gold and silver in mountains in Florida. As a result of what he said, some early maps show a mountain range in Florida.

So de Soto went off to Florida looking for the gold and silver. He ended up dying of fever on the Mississippi. Other explorers dismissed the idea of finding gold in Florida and wrote instead that it was "full of bogs and poisonous fruits, barren, and the very worst country that is warmed by the sun."

Meanwhile, in Spain, the king soon found work for Cabeza, but it was not the significant position he had anticipated. Cabeza went to Paraguay to eliminate a fierce Indian tribe. The Indians had already killed the previous Spaniard sent to bring them under control.

In Paraguay, a rival group of Spaniards seeking gold and power arrested Cabeza, put him in chains, and sent him to Spain to be tried for malfeasance. He was convicted and spent six years in jail. The king took away his royal titles. Cabeza died, probably in 1556, in obscurity.

17   A Storm Kept the French from Capturing Florida

WITH A BIT OF LUCK, OR MORE PRECISELY A BIT OF BETTER weather, the French instead of the Spanish might have ended up with Florida.

In 1562 the French government selected Captain Jean Ribault to establish a colony in Florida. These French were Huguenots, or Protestants. Ribault arrived at the mouth of the St. Johns River, near the present-day city of Jacksonville. Then he sailed north to South Carolina where he established a colony.

He returned to France, telling the colonists he left behind that he would return shortly. But when he arrived in France, he found the country in the midst of a religious war so he fled to England.

While Ribault was in England he wrote a book about his exploits, *The Whole and True Discoverye of Terra Florida*. His deputy, René Laudonnière, returned to Florida and established Fort Caroline at the mouth of the St. Johns. In 1565 Ribault returned with seven ships to reinforce Laudonnière.

The Spanish first came to Florida in 1513 and tried several times to establish colonies. But the colonies failed, and the Spanish lost interest until the French arrived. The king of Spain knew that if the French took control of Florida, they would threaten other Spanish holdings.

The sea route used by the Spanish to carry gold and silver from Central and South America passed by the coast of Florida. The Catholic Spanish also considered the Protestant French to be heretics. In 1565 the Spanish sent Pedro Menéndez de Avilés to establish a colony at St. Augustine and battle the French.

He attacked the French at Fort Caroline but was driven back. The

French then mounted an attack on St. Augustine. A violent storm scattered Ribault's ships and Menéndez was able to attack an unprotected Fort Caroline. Menéndez captured Ribault and executed him at what became known as Matanzas Inlet, which means "place of slaughter." The Spanish retained control of Florida.

1671 engraving of Fort Caroline

18 The Spanish Ruled for Three Hundred Years, But Evidence Is Hard to Find

THE SPANISH, WHO CHANGED HISTORY WITH CHRISTOPHER Columbus's 1492 discovery of the New World, ruled Florida for nearly three hundred years but left amazingly little evidence they were ever here. To find proof, it is often necessary to look below the surface, digging deep to uncover artifacts, or diving in search of wrecks of Spanish ships.

But history buffs, anxious to study the artifacts and buildings of the fifteenth- and sixteenth-century Spaniards who followed Columbus across the Atlantic, can glean valuable information at various sites throughout the state. The best-known example of Spanish influence is St. Augustine, founded in 1565 by Pedro Menéndez de Avilés. The town contains scores of structures built by the Spanish.

The Castillo de San Marcos, the large fort built by the Spanish and later used by Britain, the United States, and the Confederate States, dominates the town. Construction of the fort began in 1672 and was completed in 1695. The much smaller Fort Matanzas is about ten miles south of St. Augustine at Fort Matanzas National Monument. It was there in 1565 that the Spanish massacred a French expedition and ended the possibility of French control of Florida. After the battle, the Spanish built a small fort on what became known as Rattlesnake Island.

While the Spanish made their headquarters in St. Augustine, the French were based at Fort Caroline at the mouth of the St. Johns River. They established their settlement in 1562, when Jean Ribault placed a stone column to mark France's claim. Erosion destroyed the original fort, but a reconstructed fort has been built on the site, just east of Jacksonville.

The Gonzalez-Alvarez House in St. Augustine is known as the Oldest House. It was built in 1723, apparently for a newly married couple. The Cathedral of St. Augustine, completed in 1797, is still in use on St. Augustine's downtown plaza. Also on the plaza is Government House, built in 1716 by the Spanish and still in use. The St. Francis Barracks in St. Augustine is one of the more unusual structures—a military fort named for a saint. It started as a monastery in 1724, then was converted into barracks by the British in 1764.

In 1513 Ponce de León sailed across Biscayne Bay on the first European voyage to Florida. Today, Biscayne National Park, near Miami, has a large number of shipwrecks and artifact sites.

Exactly where Hernando de Soto landed on Florida's southwest coast in 1539 is a mystery, but a de Soto National Memorial has been built near Bradenton.

The Spanish began building Fort San Marcos de Apalachee in 1739 after two earlier forts were destroyed, but construction was never finished. On the same site are the remains of two other Spanish forts.

The Spanish were active in establishing missions in north Florida as part of a program to convert the Indians. One of the missions was the Mission de San Luis in Tallahassee, built around 1655. It became the religious center for fourteen other missions in the area. Because of a threat from the British and the possibility of attack by neighboring Indians, the Spanish built a wooden fortification on the site in 1696. Today the land is owned by the state and is a major archaeological site.

The Gulf Islands National Seashore in the Panhandle resort of Gulf Breeze has a small museum with Spanish artifacts, including old maps from the Spanish period. More artifacts can be seen at the Museum of Florida History in Tallahassee. A large collection of items relating to the early exploration of Florida is also on display at the Florida Museum of Natural History on the campus of the University of Florida in Gainesville.

19 Another Independence Day: This One Was Celebrated on July 17th

JULY 17 IS JUST ANOTHER DAY TO MOST FLORIDIANS; ITS importance in Florida history has been long forgotten. On July 17, 1821, Florida gained its independence from Spain, which had been a great power but had fallen on hard times. The United States had already acquired the giant Louisiana Purchase, making Florida an island of foreign control. Under pressure, Spain agreed to give up control of Florida.

General Andrew Jackson, the hero of the War of 1812, became governor of the new territory and with a contingent of troops left his home in Tennessee for Pensacola. On July 17, he arrived in Pensacola for a ceremony between the Spanish and Americans. Jackson did not want to humiliate the Spanish, so he kept the ceremony small. The Spanish paraded in front of the government house shortly after dawn. At eight A.M., a battalion of United States infantry arrived and formed in the public square.

At ten A.M., Jackson and his aides arrived and went to the Spanish headquarters. The ceremony giving Florida to the United States took only a few moments. The Spanish troops then left for their voyage from Florida, and the American flag was raised.

In his new role, Jackson held civilian and military powers that were so great that even Jackson was uneasy. He wrote, "I am clothed with powers that no one under a republic ought to possess, and which I trust will never be given to any man again." Even though he was the first governor (Jacksonville is named for him) Jackson came to dislike both Florida and his job and quickly resigned to return to Tennessee.

20 America Got a President While Florida Got a King

WHEN GEORGE WASHINGTON BECAME THE FIRST PRESIDENT of the United States in 1789, there were celebrations throughout the young nation. In Florida, the citizens were celebrating something entirely different. As democracy came to the United States, Floridians were honoring the ascension of Charles IV to the Spanish throne. The day-long celebration was held in St. Augustine, the largest Spanish outpost in Florida.

The city was decked out with flags, banners, and flowers. Large portraits of the new king and queen were displayed, and carpenters built a large platform decorated with carpets and tapestries. The celebration began with a brief religious ceremony at the Catholic church, then moved to the plaza where a large crowd gathered.

Soldiers fired cannons, and then church bells were rung. The governor tossed silver medals into the crowd commemorating the event and presided over a parade through town. As night approached, bonfires were lit in the plaza, and the platform in the plaza turned into a stage.

A play about a woman loved by two men was presented, and there were also private parties that continued until dawn. The governor held the most prestigious party. The next day there was a church service, followed by an afternoon siesta and more parties.

The three-day celebration ended with another parade, including a large float drawn through town by six horses. The Spanish royalty continued to rule Florida for another thirty-two years. The people of Florida did not celebrate the inauguration of a president until 1825.

FLORIDA AND THE MILITARY

21 — A Home for Franciscan Missionaries Became an Army Barracks

TODAY, THE ST. FRANCIS BARRACKS IN ST. AUGUSTINE IS THE headquarters of the Florida National Guard, standing on one of the most historic religious sites in the United States.

In 1573 an order of Franciscan missionaries arrived in St. Augustine and fifteen years later built a home. In 1605, the friars opened a seminary, the first school in what is now the United States. By 1755 a new residence for the friars was completed, a building that still stands.

When the British took control of Florida, the Spanish did not want them to acquire the church property, so it was sold to a British Catholic. The British ignored the sale and began using the structure to house soldiers. What started as a religious structure became a barracks for troops.

The British kept part of the original name, "St. Francis," a symbol of peace, and added the military term "Barracks." The British also enlarged the building. When the Spanish regained control of Florida in 1783, the Catholic Church asked for the return of the building. Spain rejected the request, and the building remained a military post.

When the United States acquired the post in 1821, U.S. Army soldiers moved in. Through the years there were several fires that damaged the building but each time it was rebuilt. During the Civil War, Confederate soldiers occupied the barracks until

St. Francis Barracks in St. Augustine

Union troops took control in 1862.

The barracks remained in federal control until 1900 when the United States abandoned it, since the government no longer needed to post troops in St. Augustine. The building was vacant for a short time, then served briefly as an orphanage in 1901.

In 1907, the state of Florida leased the building from the federal government for one dollar a year. The state used it as the headquarters for the state military department and the National Guard. Additions have been made over the past eighty years, but it is still used by the Guard. The building built as a home for missionaries has been occupied by troops from four nations.

22 Florida Declined Chance to Be Part of the Original Fifteen Colonies

HERE'S A TRIVIA QUESTION: HOW MANY ORIGINAL COLONIES were there?

Thirteen, you say. Wrong. Originally, there were seventeen colonies, but four decided not to make the trip to Philadelphia to draft the Declaration of Independence. Not surprisingly, Upper Canada and Lower Canada were two of the colonies siding with the British. Surprisingly, East Florida and West Florida also turned down the patriots and sided with the Redcoats.

For the same reason that residents of the thirteen colonies wanted the British to leave, the Floridians wanted them to stay. One of the big issues for the patriots was the presence of British troops. But the folks in Florida, always worried about possible Indian attacks, liked the idea of British troops hanging around.

As the American Revolution began, Florida became a haven for those who lived in the thirteen colonies but were loyal to the British. Land values in Florida soared as the new residents came, bringing with them their families and slaves. The British government depended on Florida to help supply its armies, bringing Floridians even greater prosperity.

There were some military battles, but the one serious attempt by the patriots to invade Florida failed. There were small-scale attacks by both loyalists and patriots along the Florida-Georgia border. The Spanish, who had once owned Florida, tried to get it back, and in 1781 captured Pensacola and eventually all of West Florida.

When the British lost the Revolution, they agreed to give both East and West Florida back to Spain. This action came as a shock to the thousands of loyal English who lived in Florida. The British government gave them some money and helped them relocate to other British colonies, primarily in the Bahamas, Jamaica, or Canada.

The British military gave up the fort at St. Augustine, where they had held three signers of the Declaration of Independence prisoner during the war. The three, all from South Carolina, reportedly spent their time singing "God Save the Thirteen States" to the tune of "God Save the King." In exchange for giving Florida to Spain, Britain kept Gibraltar, situated off the coast of Spain and now more familiar as an insurance company symbol.

23 A Future President Ignored Orders and Invaded Florida

DID THE ORDERS COME FROM THE PRESIDENT, OR DID THE general make up his own orders and thereby deliver Florida to the United States? After nearly two centuries, no one is quite sure.

In 1817, Florida belonged to Spain, an aging power unable to control its colonies. Florida became a refuge for escaped slaves, marauding Indians, and criminals. Often the criminals and Indians would commit crimes in Georgia, then slip into Florida.

Finally, Secretary of War John C. Calhoun said that General Edmund Gaines (as in Gainesville) could cross into Florida to attack Indians responsible for killing Americans. Before Gaines could carry out the orders, he was replaced by General Andrew Jackson, hero of the War of 1812.

Jackson, on white horse, inspects troops.

Jackson sent a note to President James Monroe, saying "the possession of the Floridas is desirable to the United States, and in sixty days it will be accomplished." Jackson thought the note was clear: He would invade Florida and take it for the United States. Monroe later said that was not part of his plan.

Monroe did not pay much attention to the message anyway, merely passing it on to a Cabinet member. Jackson invaded Florida and seized a Spanish fort. He captured two Seminole chiefs and two British citizens. The men were tried by a military court. The court recommended fifty lashes for one of the British citizens, but Jackson ignored the court and ordered all four executed.

The British and Spanish expressed outrage. Congress demanded an investigation of the Jackson invasion. Monroe was urged to disavow the attack and even to punish Jackson. Instead, the Monroe administration went on the offensive. Secretary of State John Quincy Adams charged that the Spanish had brought about the situation by not controlling Florida and allowing the British and Indians to use it as a base to cause trouble for the United States.

The ploy worked and the investigation ended. The Spanish position weakened, and Spain let the United States have Florida. Monroe was re-elected and John Quincy Adams and Andrew Jackson later became presidents. Still, a mystery remains: Did Monroe really intend for Jackson to invade Florida?

24 While Building a Fort and a City, William Chase Created an Industry

WILLIAM CHASE CAME TO PENSACOLA IN 1828 TO BUILD A fort. Before he finished, he had done quite a bit more. He had already built forts in Louisiana and Alabama, and the Pensacola fort should not have been any different. The government appropriated $750,000 for the work on Fort Pickens.

Chase ordered some bricks from a Mobile, Alabama, supplier but found they were very expensive and not very good. So he encouraged local firms to begin making bricks. Chase used a New Orleans bank to handle the government money, but he decided that it would be more convenient and profitable to start his own bank in Pensacola and put the government money there.

By 1834, Chase's work on the fort was coming to an end, but there was a big problem: The fort construction had become the economic basis for the town. When work stopped, so would the economy. Also, Chase was so successful at encouraging brick making that there was now a surplus of three million bricks in the town.

Chase turned to the War Department, asking for another $50,000 for some more brick laying at the fort. The department agreed, and the surplus bricks were soon gone. Chase wanted to keep things going so he secured another $106,000 to dredge the harbor a few feet deeper.

Chase could not think up any more projects to build in Pensacola, but he did not forget the city where he had close economic ties. As he built other forts along the Florida coast, he ordered his bricks from Pensacola and continued to bank there. He formed a railroad to carry the supplies he purchased for the government and became a large developer, selling nearly a million dollars worth of lots. In 1856 he resigned from the army to devote himself full time to his business interests.

When the Civil War came, Chase sided with the Confederacy. He became commander of the southern troops in Pensacola. During the war, Union troops took Fort Pickens. The Pensacola economy declined until World War I when it became a center for air training.

25 — Before They Were Finished, Florida's Forts Were Obsolete

IN THE EARLY 1800s THE FEDERAL GOVERNMENT WENT ON its first military spending binge. The idea was to provide protection from hostile nations, and the method was to construct a string of forts along the coast. The forts were huge structures with thick walls to resist cannon attacks.

When Florida became an American territory in 1821, the fort building plan was expanded to include the new, huge coastline. Four forts were built under the program in Florida, but the government did not get much for its money.

Because of developments in weaponry, delays in construction, and the forts' locations, they were obsolete before they were completed. Fort Jefferson in the Dry Tortugas and Fort Taylor on Key West were held by the Union forces during the Civil War. When the war ended, Fort Taylor was abandoned, still unfinished. Fort Jefferson became a prison, best known as the place at which Dr. Samuel Mudd served his sentence for treating John Wilkes Booth's broken leg after Booth assassinated Abraham Lincoln.

The third fort built under the program was Fort Clinch near Jacksonville. Like the others it was obsolete before it was finished. Construction began in 1847, but the fort was not finished when the Civil War began in 1861. It was occupied briefly by Confederate troops but eventually was abandoned and taken over by Union soldiers.

Fort Pickens near Pensacola was held by the Confederates until 1862 when Union forces attacked and captured Pensacola. After the war the fort became a prison and at one time held the Indian leader Geronimo.

26 Too Risky for the Mailman, So the Army Carried the Mail

AS LATE AS 1845, FLORIDA WAS SO DESOLATE AND DANGEROUS that the United States Army delivered the mail. That bothered the postmaster in the town of Pilatka, who was so upset that he fought the army for the right to deliver the mail.

The postmaster, James Cole, wrote to his supervisors that the "running of a private Express being positively prohibited, I report the matter to you, in order that you may take such steps, as you may deem proper to prevent it, and prosecute the offenders."

The route ran between Pilatka—now spelled Palatka—and Fort Brooke, now named Tampa. At the time Palatka was one of Florida's biggest cities and a shipping center. At first, the Post Office Department liked the idea of having the army deliver the mail. The army opened the route in 1841 and things went well until 1844. That is when Cole first complained about the delivery.

Cole said the army was not carrying all of the mail. The army said it was trying, but there were too many newspapers for a man on horseback to carry. Cole had a reason for complaining about the army service; the volume of mail determined his salary.

Between 1841 and 1843, Cole made $574. In 1844 and 1845, he earned just twenty-five dollars. During the 1841–1842 period the Second Seminole War was raging, and that meant lots of mail coming into Florida. When the war ended, the mail declined and so did Cole's salary.

The exchanges between the post office and the army continued until early 1845 when the post office opened its own route between Palatka and Fort Brooke. The army grew tired of the controversy. A letter from the acting adjutant general stated, "The express [army mail between St. Augustine and Tampa Bay] gives me so much trouble with the Post Office Departments—being against the letter of the law and deemed not longer absolutely necessary." The adjutant general ordered it dropped.

The army was unhappy about the service provided by the post office. An officer based in Florida complained, "We are left in a sad predicament in respect to correspondence. The mail from Fort Brooke reaches Palatka in four days and for eleven days thereafter it is moving in circles within thirty-two miles of this place before we receive or confiscate it."

IN EARLY 1898 WAR FEVER SWEPT THROUGH MUCH OF THE United States. Newspaper editorials and politicians advocated a war with Spain to secure the independence of Cuba from Spain. In Florida, the mood was very different. Many Florida newspapers, politicians, and citizens opposed the war. They thought if Cuba became free of Spain it would then become part of the United States. That could have spelled disaster for Florida's economy. Cuba produced many of the same products as Florida, including cigars and oranges, and could produce the goods more cheaply. Cuba could also threaten Florida's growing tourist trade.

Floridians were also worried that Florida would become a target if war broke out. *The Jacksonville Times Union and Citizen* asked that the army begin erecting fortifications along the coast to protect the state from Spanish attack. Miami and Tampa also asked for fortifications. Guns were emplaced on islands in Tampa Bay to defend the port. Finally on April 4, 1898, the army announced that it would erect defenses near all of the major Florida coastal cities.

President William McKinley asked for a war declaration on April 11, and four days later troops began arriving in Tampa. The state that did not want the war became the military headquarters and launching place for the invasion of Cuba.

The troops brought prosperity to Tampa. The military established a headquarters in the beautiful Tampa Bay Hotel. The city's population went from twenty-five thousand to sixty-five thousand. Other cities, including Miami, Jacksonville, and St. Augustine argued that troops should also be stationed in their cities.

Camps were set up in Lakeland, Jacksonville, Fernandina, and Miami.

Soldiers doing laundry at Tampa camp

One soldier found Miami so hot and miserable that he wrote, "If I owned both Miami and Hell, I'd sell Miami and go to live in Hell." The Miami and Fernandina camps were quickly shut down.

On April 25, something happened in Washington to turn Floridians into backers of the war. Congress passed the Platt Amendment stating that Cuba would not be annexed to the United States after the war. It was just what the Floridians wanted.

28 In the Race for Military Glory, Florida's Soldiers Were Left Behind

WHEN IT CAME TO WARS, FLORIDA WAS NOT HAVING MUCH luck. In the American Revolution, Florida sided with the British. In the Civil War, Florida fought with the Confederacy.

Along came the Spanish American War and a chance for Florida to go with a winner. But although Florida was the base for the military effort to take Cuba from the Spanish, Floridians bungled their shot at military glory. When war came in 1898, Florida was asked to provide twelve companies of soldiers. The Florida Guard had twenty companies throughout the state, and every single man was eager to fight in a war where the chance of death in battle was very small and the opportunity for glory great.

Governor William Bloxham thought he had a solution—the twenty companies could combine into twelve companies. But each company represented a city, and not one wanted to be combined with that of another city. The governor delayed as long as he could, but finally selected the twelve companies. In late May of 1898, one thousand men began training in Tampa.

Three weeks later American soldiers left for Cuba, but the Florida troops were not on the boat. With the onset of the summer rains, their camp became a swamp and they began to realize that the war would be over before they ever left Tampa. A handful of the soldiers were used in an engineering unit that actually got to Cuba. But more Floridians spent time at a camp in Alabama. Morale fell, and the men began to seek discharges. The war ended in August, just four months after it started.

Most of the Florida soldiers were mustered out in October, but the ones in Alabama remained in the army until early in 1899. Even though the Florida unit never saw action, it did have casualties. Twenty-eight men died from disease, and two were murdered; nineteen deserted. Two Floridians who were not part of the Florida regiment died in Cuba, but neither fell in battle. One died from fever, and the other from spinal meningitis.

THE LETTER WRITER WAS ANGRY: WHY, HE WROTE TO HIS congressman, was a Nazi soldier working in an Orlando laundry, standing next to patriotic American women? The answer was simple: The U.S. government placed a prisoner-of-war camp in Orlando, and prisoners were allowed to work outside the camp. POW camps were established throughout Florida during World War II, growing in population as the Allies conquered more territory and captured huge numbers of prisoners.

The main POW camp in Florida was established at Camp Blanding near Starke, about forty miles south of Jacksonville. At first it housed what were called enemy aliens—Germans from the United States and Latin America who were suspected of being sympathetic to Germany. As the Americans began to win battles, the camp began to fill with German soldiers. To relieve the overcrowding, the government set up branch camps around the state for about four thousand Germans.

A German prisoner of war at Camp Blanding

The camps usually were guarded by inexperienced American soldiers, and violence was not unusual. Members of General Erwin Rommel's Afrika Korps staged a work strike in 1943 that led to a riot and the transfer of the ringleaders to a camp in Oklahoma. There were also fights among the Germans over support for the Nazi cause.

Germans captured early in the war, when the Nazis were winning, tended to be more patriotic than those taken prisoner later, when the Germans were losing. There were a few attempts at escape, but most escapees were quickly caught. At the end of the war the camps were closed, although many of the prisoners were detained in Britain or France for more than a year.

IF YOU WERE LOOKING FOR A CHARTER BOAT IN SOUTH Florida in the 1930s, you might have come across Captain Jack Post. His boat, *Echoes of the Past,* operated out of Miami. He and his wife lived in a small house and nothing seemed out of the ordinary.

Captain Jack even served as a voter registration clerk. During the Depression, Jack's charter-boat business declined. He sold his boat and went to work as a cook near the Opa-Locka Naval Air Station.

That is where Jack Post worked in 1941 when his past caught up with him. Jack Post was really Carl Hermann Schroetter. He moved to the United States from Germany in 1913 and became a citizen. He adopted the alias Jack Post when he moved to Miami in 1930.

While living in Miami, he made five trips to Germany and kept in contact with a Karl Ludwig in New York. In 1941 the FBI cracked a Nazi spy ring that operated throughout the country. Ludwig was identified as the leader of the ring. Jack Post was arrested in the fall of 1941 for espionage and held on twenty-five thousand dollars bail.

The government said Post provided the Nazis with information about the Naval Air Station and shipping out of Miami. Post said he was forced into spying by the Nazis and was worried that if he said no, something might happen to his sister in Germany. He pointed out that he refused to help Ludwig flee the country. Did that not prove his innocence? He testified that he was "pushed into the case . . . to protect somebody's life."

Post was convicted and sentenced to ten years in prison in 1942. Pearl Harbor had been attacked three months earlier, and nobody was in a mood to go easy on a spy. Still, if Post had been arrested while America was at war, he could have been executed.

The sentence was too much for Post. Just ten days after he entered the Atlanta prison he slashed his wrists with a part from a radio, then hanged himself with a bed sheet in his cell. There were other more sensational spy cases, and Post was quickly forgotten. The question remains: Was he a traitor to his adopted country or simply trying to protect his sister?

31 Honoring the British Pilots Who Lost Their Lives in Florida

FOR HALF A CENTURY, ON REMEMBRANCE SUNDAY IN November, there has been a small ceremony in a Miami cemetery. A parade, a speech by a British official, and the firing of a military salute mark the day. On Memorial Day, there has been a similar ceremony for fifty years at a cemetery in Arcadia.

During World War II, hundreds of British airmen trained in Florida, where training could be held year-round. A number of the trainees were killed in crashes. British policy called for burying the war dead where they died rather than shipping the bodies back to England.

Twenty-three British flyers were buried in Arcadia—the site of one training base—and thirteen were buried in Miami. The British government placed headstones engraved with the Royal Air Force emblem and an epitaph written by each family on each grave.

The Rotary Club of Arcadia agreed to maintain the graves there and organize the observance, placing British flags on the graves once a year. Representatives from Great Britain still attend the ceremony each year.

32 The Nazis Land in Florida to Start a Campaign of Sabotage

ON JUNE 13, 1942, FOUR GERMAN SOLDIERS LANDED ON A beach south of Jacksonville, wearing Nazi-furnished swimwear and playing with a beach ball provided by the Nazis. They carried a hundred thousand dollars in cash to finance their assignment: to blow up power plants and factories and try to create support for the Reich among German-Americans. The four Germans were put ashore near Jacksonville by a U-boat and given instructions to "cover" their landing by appearing to be tourists enjoying the beach.

They boarded buses in Jacksonville and made their way north—two suntanned saboteurs were bound for Chicago and two for Washington, D.C. In those cities they were to meet two other pairs of German agents who had landed on Long Island simultaneously with the Florida landing. Neither rendezvous took place. Instead, FBI agents arrested the German soldiers.

One of the Germans on the northern leg of the mission called the FBI and turned in the entire group. A secret military trial was held, and all eight were sentenced to death. President Franklin Roosevelt commuted the sentences of two of the Germans who cooperated with the FBI. Less than six weeks after they landed, six of the Germans were shot. No news of their mission was released to the American public until after the war ended.

THE CIVIL WAR

33 With Few Reservations,
Florida Left the Union

LATE IN 1860, WILLIAM WOODRUFF AND ISAAC RUTLAND made the long trip from Orlando to Tallahassee to take part in the Florida secession convention. Abraham Lincoln had been elected president, and throughout the South there were cries to leave the Union. In Florida the secession furor was very loud, although Woodruff and Rutland were among the small number who favored delay.

The background of the convention delegates varied widely. Only ten percent were native Floridians; the rest were from sixteen other states, the Bahamas, and Ireland. Nearly a third were natives of Georgia, another state in a rush to leave the Union.

A third were farmers, and lawyers, merchants, and physicians each accounted for ten percent. Woodruff and Rutland were farmers. The richest delegate was E. E. Simpson of north Florida, who was worth $2.5 million. The poorest was Daniel McLean of Washington County in the Panhandle, with a net worth of $200. Woodruff was worth $730. Rutland had assets of nearly $4,000. Neither Woodruff nor Rutland owned slaves. James H. Chandler, a preacher who represented Volusia County, was worth about $5,000 and owned six slaves. William B. Yates, a Brevard County farmer, was worth $1,300 and owned no slaves.

Yates and Chandler favored immediate secession, and there was little doubt which way the overwhelming majority of the sixty-nine delegates would vote. Woodruff, Rutland, and others who favored delaying secession were overwhelmed. Time after time they introduced delaying amendments, only to have them voted down. On January 10, 1861, the convention voted 62 to 7 to leave the Union and join the Confederacy.

WHEN THE CIVIL WAR STARTED, MOST OF FLORIDA'S SEV-enty thousand white residents were enthusiastic. They did not believe the North would fight to maintain the Union, and even if war did come the South was sure to win quickly. However, when the war started, Florida was the state most neglected by the Confederate States of America.

Florida Governor John Milton wrote to Confederate Secretary of War Judah P. Benjamin in 1861: "Florida wants arms. She has never received a musket from the Confederate State. . . . Can she get some?" Not only did Florida not receive any guns, the secretary did not even bother to answer the letter.

As the Florida troops moved into other Confederate states to fight Yankees, the state was left virtually unprotected. Local militia could not defend the thirteen-hundred mile coastline. Union troops held a number of ports throughout the war and took control of Pensacola and Jacksonville when the Confederates abandoned them.

By 1863 morale had fallen so low that there was talk of Florida's rejoining the Union. When Union troops marched into Jacksonville the mayor said that it was "useless to attempt a defense of the city." After Union troops took the city, pro-Union rallies were held. The Union set up a naval blockade around Florida that cut off vital supplies. As the war dragged on, some residents did not have enough food.

Abraham Lincoln took note of what was happening and dispatched his secretary, John Hay, to entice Florida into rejoining the Union. Hay's mission looked promising until about fifty-five hundred Union soldiers were defeated in the Battle of Olustee on February 20, 1864. The plan to get Florida back into the Union in 1864 failed. Tallahassee was the only Confederate capital east of the Mississippi that Union troops did not capture.

35   C.S.S. *Florida* Saw Plenty of Action, But Never Saw Florida

THE CONFEDERATE NAVY HAD A PROBLEM IN 1861: NO SHIPS and no place to build them. The Confederate ports where war ships might have been built were under constant threat from Union ships. So the Confederates contracted in England and France to have ships built there.

The British had announced they would not build ships for the South.

But British ship builders began construction of a warship in 1861, claiming that it was actually being built for the Italian Navy. Although the Italians denied they had ordered a ship, construction went ahead. It was originally named the *Orento* so that people would think it was for Italy.

The *Orento* sailed from Liverpool for Nassau where the British government in Nassau pretended to be alarmed and held the ship briefly until a jury ordered it released. The *Orento* name was dropped and it became the C.S.S. *Florida*, the most famous wooden ship in the Confederate Navy.

The *Florida* became one of the South's greatest threats to the Union, roaming throughout the Atlantic capturing and sinking Union ships. In October 1864 she sailed from the Atlantic on a voyage to the Pacific to capture Union whaling ships. While the *Florida* was anchored in a Brazilian port, Union ships showed up.

The Brazilian Navy feared a battle between the Confederates and the Union flotilla would erupt in the port and placed a ship between the *Florida* and the Union ships. The U.S.S. *Wachusett* sailed around the Brazilian ship in an attempt to ram the Confederate ship. The *Florida* was hit and sustained enough damage to force its surrender. While being towed, the *Florida* sank. During its service it captured nearly seventy-five ships but never made port in Florida.

36   Confederate Armies Turned to Florida to Feed the Soldiers

FLORIDA SENT FIFTEEN THOUSAND MEN TO FIGHT FOR THE Confederacy, just two percent of the total Confederate army. More important than the soldiers were the thousands of heads of cattle Florida sent to keep the Confederate Army from starving. In the first year of the war, the Confederate army had few problems with food. The South was primarily an agricultural region, and Union armies had not entered most of the Confederacy.

By 1862, Confederate defeats in Tennessee began to create beef shortages for the army. Two thirds of the cows for Braxton Bragg's army came from Tennessee, and the rest came from Virginia and Florida. In 1863 the South faced a serious cattle shortage. The Confederate Army of Tennessee was only getting half the beef it needed.

The army turned to Florida for help. For the first time, Confederate commissary agents fanned out across the state. In April 1863 about three thousand Florida cows arrived to help feed the Army of Tennessee. But events on the Mississippi River created even more of a demand. As Union forces captured ports along the river, it became more difficult for the

Confederacy to obtain cattle from Texas.

Officials estimated that Florida would need to ship one thousand cows a week to feed one of the South's two major armies. But finding that many cows was difficult. Florida was isolated with a miserable transportation system, and the cows had to be herded to Madison, a small town in north Florida.

Many Florida ranchers did not want to sell their cows to the government. They distrusted the value of Confederate money and had the option of selling their cows to Union buyers. Rounding up Florida cattle was often dangerous, with snakes, sudden storms, and marshes making roundups dangerous.

Florida was unable to make up for the shortages. The Army of Tennessee was slowly starving and being pushed from Tennessee. By the fall of 1863, the army had fallen back to Georgia. Florida contributed thirty thousand head of cattle in 1863, but only about twenty thousand in 1864. In all, Florida contributed about seventy-five thousand cows to help feed the Confederate Army, but it was not enough.

37 A Confederate Officer's Story: Finding Glory and Death in War

IN EARLY 1860, JOHN PEARSON BECAME CONVINCED THAT the Civil War was coming. He purchased 125 rifles and 100 revolvers and went to work organizing a company of soldiers in north Florida to fight for the Confederacy.

Pearson was a prosperous businessman in the tiny community of Orange Springs, where he operated a sawmill, hotel, and cattle ranch. He also raised cotton and owned twenty slaves who worked his land.

He selected his men with care, limiting enrollment to those who were in good health. His unit elected him captain, and when the war began, Pearson and his men were sent to Tampa for what was supposed to be an easy assignment. He assumed command of Tampa's Fort Brooke and assisted blockade runners bringing goods from England to the Confederacy.

Soon after his arrival, a Union ship anchored off Tampa and demanded that Pearson surrender the town. He refused, and the Union ship began shelling the town. Pearson answered with his shore batteries. The Union fleet withdrew and Pearson's fame began to spread.

He and his men became known as the Oklawaha Rangers. At one point, when a federal ship was off Tampa, he had some of his soldiers put on disguises, including a few dresses, to lure the sailors to shore. It worked, and a launch was sent to bring Union sailors ashore. When they were in range, the soldiers opened fire, hitting four sailors.

In 1863 Pearson and his men were ordered to Jacksonville. Early in 1864, with the help of Pearson's unit, the Confederates won at Olustee. Pearson was promoted to lieutenant colonel and ordered to Virginia to join General Robert E. Lee.

In his first encounter with Union troops in Virginia, Pearson was wounded and hospitalized for nearly two months. In August 1864, as Grant closed in around Richmond, Pearson's unit faced its toughest fighting. Pearson was told to attack the Union fortifications. As he led the charge he was shot in the chest. The wound was serious, and three days later he resigned his commission.

After resting for several weeks, he left for his Florida home. He was still weak, and on September 30, 1864, he died in Augusta, Georgia. His men continued their fight until they surrendered to Grant at Appomattox Court House in 1865.

38 With the Southern Cause Lost, the Secretary of War Slipped Away

BEFORE THE CIVIL WAR JOHN BRECKINRIDGE WAS VICE PRESident of the United States and a Democratic nominee for president. When he came through Florida in 1865 he was a man on the run, staying one step ahead of the Union troops trying to capture him.

Breckinridge served as the Confederate Secretary of War in the final weeks of the Confederacy, then fled Richmond with other government officials as the Union army closed in. He faced treason charges if caught and feared that he might be executed.

Breckinridge disguised himself and traveled under the name "Colonel Cabell." Accompanied by his two sons and several other men, he moved into Florida in May and worked his way south. Near Live Oak and Gainesville, they spent their nights sleeping on tavern floors.

Breckinridge continued down the Florida peninsula toward Cuba. He and his party moved through Ocala to Umatilla, where they purchased supplies for the trip up the St. Johns River. They slept in boats in the middle of the river to avoid the mosquitoes.

From the St. Johns River they hauled their small boat overland to the Indian River, a trip that took three days. They spent the night at Cape Canaveral, where to Breckinridge's surprise the mosquitoes were worse than on the St. Johns. At the Indian River Inlet they slipped past a federal guard post and entered the Atlantic Ocean. Because their boat was so small, they were forced to stay close to the shore.

The boat was not very seaworthy, so Breckinridge decided to find a larger vessel. He sighted a larger boat more seaworthy than his, gave chase, and at gunpoint forced the frightened passengers to exchange boats. After that the trip got even tougher.

They exchanged shots with pirates, and on the way to Cuba nearly drowned in the rough seas. Finally, after several days they reached Cuba where sympathetic Spanish officials gave Breckinridge and his men a hero's welcome. From there Breckinridge sailed for England and finally made his way to Canada.

39 He Was Lovable and Kind, but He Helped Plot an Assassination

TO HIS SISTER, LEWIS POWELL WAS "LOVABLE, SWEET, KIND." To his neighbors in the north Florida town of Live Oak, he was tender-hearted. His father, George, thought Lewis might end up working for the church. No one expected Powell to end up dangling from the end of a rope or to help change the course of history.

Lewis Powell was one of the men who conspired with John Wilkes Booth to assassinate Abraham Lincoln. Powell joined the Confederate Army in 1861, was wounded and captured at Gettysburg, escaped from the hospital, and returned to Virginia to rejoin the Confederates.

Lewis Powell

Early in 1865 he deserted, rode through the Union lines, and took an oath of loyalty to the United States. He swore his name was Lewis Payne. He then went to Baltimore, where an acquaintance introduced him to the actor John Wilkes Booth. Booth later briefed Lewis on a plan to kidnap Lincoln, and hold him for ransom until the North released Confederate prisoners of war.

Booth was to be the brains and Lewis, a strong man of limited intelligence, the brawn of what evolved into an assassination plan. The kidnapping plan failed to materialize, and instead Booth decided to kill Lincoln, Vice President Andrew

Johnson, and Secretary of State William Seward.

On the night of April 14, 1865, Booth went to the theater to kill Lincoln. Lewis entered Seward's house pretending to deliver medicine, ran upstairs to Seward's bedroom, and stabbed him a number of times. Seward's sons forced Lewis to flee, and he was later arrested by Union officers.

The secretary eventually recovered. Lewis' trial was brief. On July 7, 1865, he was executed in Washington as a huge crowd watched. Lewis's father, traveling to Washington to visit his son, got word of the execution in Jacksonville. Soon after, the family moved to Geneva, a small community near Orlando, to escape the attention that their infamous son brought them.

40 Eight Years, Eight Governors, Through Florida's Revolving Door

IN THE NINETEENTH CENTURY, FLORIDA HAD EIGHT GOV-
ernors in eight years. There were elected governors, acting governors, and one self-appointed governor. The strange chain of events began in 1865, when John Milton was governor. Milton was a true supporter of the Confederacy, and when the end came, Milton couldn't take it anymore. On April 1, 1865, he committed suicide, leaving behind a final message to the legislature: "Death would be preferable to reunion."

Abraham Allison was president of the Florida Senate when Milton died. He became acting governor at just the wrong time. Six weeks after he took over, he was arrested by federal troops and put in prison for six months.

President Andrew Johnson appointed William Marvin as governor, but Marvin held the job for only six months before resigning and returning to New York. David Walker was next, winning an election without opposition and serving two and one half years before retiring.

That's when Harrison Reed, a Republican, was elected governor. He had been in office only a few months when members of his own party tried to oust him. Then, Lieutenant Governor William Gleason made his move. Gleason proclaimed himself governor and began signing documents from his hotel headquarters.

Gleason had overplayed his hand. Reed went to court claiming that not only wasn't Gleason the governor but he had not been a state resident long enough to be lieutenant governor. The court agreed, and Gleason was removed as governor and lieutenant governor.

In 1872 there was another attempt to remove Reed from office. This time, Samuel T. Day stepped forward and claimed to be governor. Reed had gone to his Jacksonville farm when Day occupied the governor's office. Day appointed some state officials and held the job for nearly three months. Then he made the mistake of leaving Tallahassee to attend a meeting. Reed showed up, retook the governor's office, and asked the court for an opinion. The court supported Reed.

The next governor, Ossian Bingley Hart, served almost an entire year before dying of pneumonia. Hart merits a historical footnote only because he was the first Florida native elected governor.

SCHOOL DAYS

One-Room Schoolhouse Times Were Tough for Teachers

IN 1897 SUSAN SANDERS FINISHED HER TEACHER TRAINING in Iowa, and at the age of twenty-one left her home to begin her career. She decided to move to Palm Beach, where her brother had moved nearly a decade before. Sanders arrived at the railroad station in Stuart and had to walk to her new home.

She boarded in one large room with the Lee family, which consisted of the parents and six children. She was assigned to sleep with their twelve-year-old daughter in one corner of the room. She taught in a one-room shack and was paid forty dollars per month.

Women in the area sold quilts to raise the two hundred dollars necessary to buy the lumber to build a school building. When the lumber arrived from Jacksonville, the men built the school.

One of the early teachers was Hattie Gale, who was sixteen when she taught her first class in 1886 near Palm Beach. She was about the same age as some of her students and decided to return to school to get more education. She came back to Florida several years later with her new husband.

Teacher Hattie Carpenter came to Florida in 1900. She settled in Miami and took the examination for her teaching certificate. She later wrote, "I took the examination that spring and I guess I had the lowest grade ever given any human being down there. . . . They told me to trace a water route from Kissimmee to Key West. I couldn't even pronounce Kissimmee, and I didn't know where it was anyway. . . . Somehow they gave me a certificate, I don't think I deserved it."

But Carpenter had written some articles about Florida for an Ohio newspaper. The articles were not very flattering, and local residents demanded she be fired. Instead she was transferred to a new school in Miami. To maintain discipline, she told her students to act as though they were hunting deer at all times. Eventually Carpenter became principal of the school. But after three years she was discouraged with the lack of resources and quit education to become a reporter for the *Miami Metropolis*.

42 When It Came to Schools, Florida Was a Slow Learner

FLORIDA SCHOOLS HAVE COME A LONG WAY SINCE THE 1901 school year, when just 136 high school diplomas were handed out in the entire state. Now, more than eighty thousand seniors earn their degrees each year. When Florida became a territory in 1822, huge sections of the state were set aside for lease or sale to finance a public school system.

It was a fine idea, but nobody started any public schools. The state's first free public school was finally opened in St. Augustine in 1831, but it soon folded for lack of money. There was great resistance to public schools from wealthy Floridians who could afford to educate their own children, and who saw no reason to pay to educate anyone else's. In 1839 another attempt was made to set up a public school system. The territorial government set aside tax money for public schools, but once again no one took advantage of the cash.

Another attempt in 1844 also failed. Somebody came up with the idea of using lotteries to finance public education. The territorial government approved the lottery idea, but it never got off the ground. Now history is repeating itself, as the state uses a lottery to help finance education.

43 The Bidding Was Fierce to Win Rollins College

WHEN THE REVEREND EDWARD HOOKER ARRIVED IN Winter Park in 1884 to set up a Congregational Church, he wasn't impressed. There was only one store in town, and the few residents were primarily illiterate swamp dwellers. Hooker thought a college would be the answer and asked his brothers in the Congregational Church to establish one in Florida.

They said yes, and the search was on for a site. A college could give a small community a sense of identity, assure its survival, and increase property values. The smaller the town, the harder it pushed to secure a college.

In this case, there were five bidders. Mount Dora offered ten acres near the water and seven hundred additional acres nearby to sell or lease, with a total value of $35,564. Daytona offered $20,000 and an oceanfront site. Jacksonville's offer was just $13,000 plus a site. Orange City could come up with only $10,000.

Then it was Winter Park's turn. The town offered $125,000 in land and cash. Winter Park, smallest of the five, was the winner. The college was named for its largest benefactor, Alonzo Rollins, and opened on November 4, 1885.

The students were taught and housed in temporary buildings while carpenters worked furiously to finish the permanent buildings.

The early Rollins college campus

The admission requirements were tough. Incoming freshman were required to have studied Latin, four books of Caesar, six orations of Cicero, Greek prose composition, French, American history, and a dozen other subjects.

44 — Delaying Tactics Hindered Florida School Integration

ON MAY 17, 1954, THE UNITED STATES SUPREME COURT ruled that school segregation was unconstitutional. The decision, *Brown v. Board of Education of Topeka*, came as a shock to the South, where school segregation was a way of life. In many Southern states there were cries of outrage, but in Florida the reaction was restrained. The state had a public school enrollment of nearly 650,000 students, including 140,000 blacks.

Most newspapers opposed the court's decision, but still urged people to remain calm. Senator George Smathers said that it would be wasteful to spend time attacking the court's decision and that there should be no "hasty decisions, no inflammatory statements based on anger or resentment."

The decision came in the middle of a battle for the Democratic gubernatorial nomination between Acting Governor Charley Johns and State

Senator LeRoy Collins. Johns announced that he had asked the attorney general to study the ruling and advise what it meant for Florida. Collins, a strong supporter of segregation, said the governor should use all his powers to ensure a segregated school system.

Most people thought it would be years before desegregation actually took place. The Florida legislature adopted tactics to delay integration. From 1954 to 1959 the legislature passed twenty-one laws designed to keep public schools segregated. They all failed. As late as 1959, a committee drafting a new state constitution urged retention of an amendment establishing separate school systems.

In the fall of 1959 Miami became the first Florida city to integrate its schools. The Miami integration was just the first step, and it was not until the mid-1960s that integration on a large scale was under way in Florida. Collins won the gubernatorial election, but once in office he turned out to be a moderate on school segregation. While other Southern governors promised to defy the courts or even to close the schools, Collins urged patience and restraint. As a result, the integration of Florida schools was smoother than in any other deep-South state.

45   Finding a Home for Florida University

FLORIDA HAS SEEN COLLEGES COME AND GO. DOZENS OF colleges have failed while others have defied the odds and continued to exist. Many of the failed colleges were established in small towns that could not support the schools.

In 1883 Florida University was created with little in the way of resources but plenty of big plans. The school was to have a college of literature and a college of medicine. The organizers pushed a bill through the legislature recognizing their school as "the university of the State and to be known as the University of Florida."

During the 1884–85 school year Florida University had seventy-nine students, including one from Georgia. There were seventy-one students in the literary college. The admission requirements were not very difficult. Candidates had to be at least twelve years old. If they were enrolling as military students they had to be at least five feet tall. "Suitable age, good morals and the payment of fees" were the only requirements for admission. Even the medical school admitted all those who met the three criteria.

A typical beginning student would choose from the following classes: Spelling, Reading, Grammar, Geography, Word Analysis, U.S. History,

Rhetoric, History of England, Elocution, American Literature, Mental Science, and Critical Reading of English Classics. Graduates had to show "good moral character, possess a good English education (Latin, Greek, German and French being also desirable), as well as a competent knowledge of the Natural Sciences."

Despite endless self-promotion, the university never did achieve success. One year the medical school had just five students. In an effort to attract more students, the medical classes were opened up to anyone who wanted to attend. Although the school was supposed to have a dental college, it never opened.

The state withdrew recognition of the school as the state university and it closed within a few years.

46 A College Student Led the Way to the Creation of Junior High Schools

UNTIL THE 1920S, SCHOOL CHILDREN KNEW ONLY TWO types of schools: the eight-year grammar school and the four-year high school. Then came J. Hooper Wise, a young graduate student at the University of Florida. He was a leader in a movement to create a third school between grammar school and high school.

Wise was working on his doctorate, and he convinced school officials to establish a model junior high school in Orlando. In 1922, Memorial Junior High School opened, one of the first junior high schools in the country. The new school offered the basic courses but added art, music, club activities, and mechanical courses.

The school had a large stage, and the auditorium could seat one thousand. For the students at Memorial there were new activities and each home room elected officers. The school had a new system of discipline. A student who misbehaved received a discipline card. A student who got six cards received a warning from the principal. Nine discipline cards and the student had a choice: suspension and facing parents, or a paddling.

47 Black Teachers Suffered along with Black Students

THE SYSTEM OF SEGREGATED SCHOOLS EXISTED IN FLORIDA until the 1960s. For black students, it meant second-class buildings, buses, books, and often shorter school terms than those of their white counterparts. The system was also hard on black teachers who earned far less than white teachers in Florida.

In 1937 Brevard County, a typical Florida county, had two pay formulas—one for white teachers, the other for black teachers. The minimum a white teacher could receive was one hundred dollars a month for an eight-month-term. But the minimum a black teacher could earn was fifty dollars a month, half of what white teachers were guaranteed.

Usually, white teachers received more than the a hundred dollars a month. The state gave the counties eight hundred dollars a year per teacher. The counties were supposed to add to that to make teaching more attractive. Some did add money, and some did not.

One black teacher, John Gilbert, was tired of the discrimination and filed suit to stop the unequal pay. Gilbert received help from the national headquarters of the National Association for the Advancement of Colored People. Walter White, head of the NAACP, assigned future Supreme Court Justice Thurgood Marshall to the case.

Marshall traveled to Brevard County to help with the case. The local school board responded to the suit by firing Gilbert. The Florida Supreme Court held that because Gilbert was no longer a teacher, he could not sue. The NAACP considered taking the case to a federal court, but because Gilbert had been fired, the case had become more difficult. The NAACP was looking for a discrimination case that would provide a clear victory. Gilbert became an insurance salesman, but he inspired other black teachers to file suit.

In 1941 a federal judge ruled that black teachers should receive equal pay. But now opposition came from another group. The Florida Education Association came forward to oppose equal pay for black teachers. The FEA, which represented the states white teachers, maintained that if blacks were paid more, white teachers would receive less. But the appeal of the FEA was rejected, and one by one Florida counties began paying black teachers the same as white teachers.

48 A Scandal Cost Ocala the University of Florida

IF THE PIANO TEACHER HADN'T CAUGHT THE EYE OF GILBERT Dennis Kingsbury, the University of Florida might be in Ocala instead of Gainesville. Kingsbury announced in 1852 that he planned to start a college in Ocala. Ocala merchants agreed to raise six thousand dollars for the school, and Kingsbury began recruiting students. He had about sixty when school opened. But the merchants were a tad slow coming up with cash.

When the contractor began demanding his money, Kingsbury

searched for another plan. His new idea was to let the state of Florida pick up the tab. The U.S. government had passed legislation allowing Florida to sell land to pay for institutions of higher learning. All Kingsbury needed was for the state to give him any money it had accumulated from land sales.

Because Kingsbury's school was funded by the state, it became a state institution. Kingsbury was named principal of the newly named East Florida Seminary in Ocala. Everything was going well at the Ocala school until Anna Underwood arrived. She had been hired by Kingsbury to teach piano, but apparently there was more to their relationship than music.

Soon, rumors swept through the town that the two were having an immoral relationship. Kingsbury and Underwood denied it. Later, Underwood gave birth to a child, which lent some credence to the rumors. In the wake of the scandal Kingsbury was forced to resign from the Ocala school and leave the state. Three faculty members also resigned, leaving the school with students but no teachers.

The school limped along until the end of the Civil War, but Kingsbury had been the force behind its success. Without him, East Florida Seminary began to die. In 1866 state Senator James Roper of Gainesville pushed to have the school moved to his town. When he offered property, the state agreed and the East Florida Seminary moved in that same year. the name was later changed to the University of Florida.

The campus plan for the University of Florida

WHEN THE FLORIDA STATE UNIVERSITY FOOTBALL TEAM TAKES the field for home games, the players are led by its mascot, Chief Osceola, who rides out onto the field astride a beautiful horse. Osceola was an Indian leader who successfully battled United States troops in the Seminole Wars. He was captured in 1837 near St. Augustine and died in captivity the following year.

But there are some striking differences between the real Osceola and FSU's Chief Osceola. First, Osceola was never a chief. He did lead some Indians but never achieved the rank of chief.

The Osceola at FSU rides a marvelous horse onto the field. The real Osceola never owned a horse. Apparently the first time he rode a horse was when he was thirty-three years old and the United States Army put him on a horse for the seven-mile trip to St. Augustine.

The Osceola at FSU wears a war bonnet with colorful feathers. The real Osceola wore a tightly wrapped turban on his head, sometimes with white or black ostrich feathers. Part of the opening ceremony at FSU games involves Osceola hurling a spear into the ground. It looks great, but it never happened. The real Osceola used a more effective weapon—a gun.

At FSU Osceola wears an outfit right out of a western movie. In real life he wore a kind of shirt that came to his knees. From the knees down his legs were covered by leggings, usually made of leather or wool. The government eventually defeated the Seminoles and resettled most of them in Oklahoma. The FSU Indian looks a lot like an Oklahoman Indian, rather than a Florida Indian.

A WRITER'S PARADISE

**An Old English Rhyme Told of
Florida for the First Time**

HUNDREDS OF BOOKS HAVE BEEN WRITTEN ABOUT FLORIDA
since Escalante de Fonteneda published his story of being shipwrecked
four hundred years ago.

In the Bodleian Library at Oxford University in England there is what
is believed to be the first poem about Florida. It is written in longhand
and apparently was written in the early 1600s.

> And as I walked toward St. Pauls
> I met a friend of myne
> Who took {me} by the hand and sayde,
> "Com drynk a pynt of wyne,
> Wher you shall here
> Such news, I fere,
> As you abrode will compell,
>   With hy!
> Have you not hard of Floryda,
> A countree far bywest?
> Where savage pepell planted are
> By nature and be hest,
> Who in the mold find glysterynge gold
> And yt for tryfels sell:
>   With hy!
> Ye all along the water syde,
> Wher yt doth eb and flowe
> Are turkeyse found, and wher also
> Do perles in oysteres growe:
> And on the land do cedars stand
> Whose bewty do excell,
> With hy! wunnot a wallet do well?"

51 — Stowe Battled Slavery, Then Promoted Florida Tourism

HARRIET BEECHER STOWE, WHO WROTE *UNCLE TOM'S CABIN*, the emotional story of a slave's life, was also one of Florida's pioneers. After the Civil War, Stowe's son, Fred, recovering from a wound suffered at Gettysburg, moved to Florida and planted orange trees on the St. Johns. Stowe came to visit and fell in love with Florida.

She built a cottage and began spending winters there. She also established a school and became active in church work. She invited her old friends to visit, including William Cullen Bryant and Mark Twain. In 1872

Harriet Beecher Stowes home in Mandarin

Stowe began to write travel articles about Florida. They became a book entitled *Palmetto Leaves*. It was the first widespread promotion for Florida, and within a few years the tourists were coming regularly to north Florida, many visiting Stowe's home.

The visits became a distraction to her and her family. After her husband's death in 1886 she sold her Florida property and returned to Connecticut. The tourists continued to come to Florida in increasing numbers.

52 — Florida Provided the Setting and Inspiration for Many Authors

FOR MORE THAN FOUR CENTURIES FLORIDA HAS BEEN THE setting for hundreds of books. The first book about Florida was written by Escalante de Fonteneda, who was shipwrecked in 1545, spent seventeen years living among the Indians, and wrote his memoirs about life in Florida.

Jacques LeMoyne came to Florida about the time Fonteneda left. He not only wrote about life among the Indians of Florida but drew scores of pictures of the Indians. His pictures gave Europeans one of the first looks at the Indians.

In the 1600s Jonathan Dickinson described being shipwrecked in Florida in his book, which became a best seller in England. Stephen Crane, best known for writing *The Red Badge of Courage,* was on board a ship that wrecked off the coast of New Smyrna in 1897. A small lifeboat took him toward Daytona Beach, then broke up as it reached the shore. He wrote about the experience in *The Open Boat.*

Poet Sidney Lanier wrote pieces to promote tourism in Florida, and Harriet Beecher Stowe, best known for *Uncle Tom's Cabin,* moved to Florida after the Civil War and wrote of its beauty. In the 20th century Florida has been home to some of the country's best writers. Majorie Kinnan Rawlings wrote *The Yearling,* which won the Pulitzer Prize in 1939. She followed that with *Cross Creek* in 1942. Both were set in central Florida.

The same year Rawlings moved to Florida, Earnest Hemingway arrived in Key West. He wrote several books in Florida, but only one, *To Have and Have Not,* is set in Florida.

Zora Neale Hurston of Eatonville achieved initial success as an author but died forgotten and broke. Only recently have her writings once again been recognized. Tennessee Williams also called Key West home. Florida was the setting for most of John D. MacDonald's books, including his best seller *Condominium.*

53 The Creator of Sleepy Hollow Helped Promote a Florida Governor

WASHINGTON IRVING IS BEST KNOWN AS THE AUTHOR OF *The Headless Horseman* or *The Legend of Sleepy Hollow.* He also provided a major boost to the political career of a Florida governor, creating what might be called "The Legend of William Duval."

Duval became the first territorial governor of Florida in 1822 and held the post for nearly twelve years. Duval County in northeast Florida is named for him. Although he spelled his name DuVal, it is generally written as Duval.

While serving as governor Duval met Irving, perhaps the nation's leading author. Irving was very impressed and made Duval the main character in two stories he wrote. In one story Duval is cast as Ralph Ringwood, who rises from backwoods farm boy to become wealthy and powerful. Ringwood leaves home as a boy and ventures into the wilds of Kentucky, where he kills a bear and lives on his own. He later studies law and enters politics. Duval did leave home for Kentucky at the age of fourteen, then studied law.

Little else is known of Duval's early life, but the Irving account has generally been accepted as accurate, although it is an over-flattering portrait. In Irving's second story, set in Florida, he drops the name Ringwood and uses Duval. In this story Duval is once again a hero. In a showdown with the Indians, Duval is pictured as riding into the Indian camp and refusing to back down when an Indian chief threatens him with a knife. The Indians, overwhelmed with Duval's resolve, back down, their spirit broken. The story was read throughout the country, and Duval became famous. But it did not help his political career in Florida.

Florida became a state in 1845, and three years later Duval ran for Congress. His opponents claimed he was a "lightweight, made famous chiefly by Washington Irving's story of Ralph Ringwood." The critics charged that Duval's early life "had its origins with Irving, not with DuVal." Duval lost the election and left Florida. He moved to Texas, where he died in 1854 at the age of seventy.

54 Sight Unseen, Coleridge Put Xanadu in Florida

In Xanadu did Kubla Khan
A stately pleasure-dome decree
Where Alph, the sacred river ran
Through caverns measureless to man
Down to a sunless sea.

In 1763 the famed botanist John Bartram passed through Florida, then a British possession. Bartram and his son, Billy, were here to observe the plants and wildlife. While the father conducted research, Billy wrote extensively in his journal about the colony.

His writing was vivid, and in 1791 he published a book about his findings. It was a success, and for the first time the world had an idea of Florida's lush vegetation and beautiful streams and rivers. William Bartram described the alligators and Indians for many people who had seen neither. The book was printed in England where the poet Wordsworth read it and liked it immensely.

He passed it along to his sister, Dorothy, who also read it and liked it. She gave the book to the poet Samuel Taylor Coleridge. He enjoyed it as much as the others. As Coleridge read about the beauty of Florida, he fell asleep. He dreamed about the streams and springs, and when he awoke, he was inspired to finish his greatest poem, "Kubla Khan."

Since Coleridge had never actually seen Florida, he did take some liberties with his description. And so his poem includes one thing Florida did not have: *"It was a miracle of rare device. A sunny pleasure-dome with caves of ice."*

55 Sidney Lanier's Skill with Words Promoted Florida Tourism

AT ONE TIME SIDNEY LANIER'S POEMS ABOUT THE SOUTH were required reading for students. The poems made him famous, if not wealthy, and that fame led him to become one of Florida's best promoters.

As a Confederate soldier Lanier spent four months in a Union prison camp, where he caught tuberculosis, which was to cut short his life. After the war he tried to earn a living by writing, but nearly starved. He turned to law, but became disenchanted and returned to writing.

In 1875 an unusual letter came from the Atlantic Coast Line Railroad. The railroad proposed to pay Lanier the very attractive sum of $125 a month, provide him with travel expenses, and allow him to wander through Florida to write a booklet about the state.

The railroad wanted a booklet to promote Florida and persuade more tourists to use its trains. There were not many attractions in Florida in 1875, so Lanier mostly described flowers and other natural wonders. The booklet also had a section aimed at people with health problems. Lanier said Florida's climate helped his condition.

The booklet was expanded into a book, *Florida: Its Scenery, Climate and History,* and became Lanier's most popular writing. It had a remarkable impact on tourism and may have been the best investment the railroad ever made. Lanier took his own advice and moved to Florida when his condition worsened. The climate improved his health and disposition temporarily, but he died in 1881 at the age of thirty-nine.

56 Zora Hurston's Star Burned Brightly, but She Died in Obscurity

ZORA NEALE HURSTON BECAME ONE OF THE FOREMOST black writers in the 1930s, but her career was tragically short. Her first novel, *Jonah's Gourd Vine,* received glowing reviews. The Eatonville native was widely honored and settled in Daytona Beach, where she wrote and taught at Bethune-Cookman College.

The fame ended suddenly, the result of a horrible mistake. In 1948, at age forty-seven, she was charged with having sexual relations with two boys. The witness, the boys' mother, later realized that Hurston was not the woman involved. Hurston was out of the coun-

Zora Neale Hurston

try at the time of the incident, but her reputation was ruined.

She wrote, "All that I have believed in has failed me." She all but stopped writing and went to work as a maid in south Florida. The wealthy family she worked for didn't know she was an author. When she wrote an article for the *Saturday Evening Post,* newspapers picked up on the famous writer working as a maid. Her embarrassed employer fired her.

Broke and alone, she moved to Ft. Pierce, living out her life in obscurity. She died of a stroke in 1960. Her friends paid for her funeral. Since her death her reputation as a writer has been restored.

57 Emerson Sought Warm Florida Air and Found Inspiration for a Poem

IN THE WINTER OF 1827 RALPH WALDO EMERSON, A RECENT graduate of Harvard University, was advised to leave Boston and head for a warmer climate. The twenty-three-year old was suffering from a lung disease that was aggravated by the cold New England winter. He moved to Charleston, South Carolina, but found it almost as cold and dreary as Boston.

He decided to push on south to Florida, which had become part of the United States only six years earlier. After growing up in puritanical Boston, St. Augustine was definitely a shock. The town was dirty and had only about one thousand residents. What surprised Emerson the most was that nobody seemed to work. He wrote to his brother, "It is a queer place. . . . What is grown here? Oranges, on which no cultivation seems to be bestowed."

He said that his primary amusement was to "stroll on the sea-beach and drive a green orange over the sand with a stick." Emerson spent less than three months in St. Augustine, then left and never returned. Back in Boston he soon became one of the country's best-known writers. He left behind several poems about St. Augustine and his recuperation, including this verse from an untitled poem:

> Farewell; and fair be all thee, gentle town.
> The prayer of those who thank thee for their life,
> The benison of those fragrant airs,
> And the simple hospitality hath blest,
> Be to thee ever as the rich perfume
> Of a good name, and pleasant memory.

58 Hemingway Thought Key West Perfect, Except for the Tourists

WHEN ERNEST HEMINGWAY STEPPED ONTO THE DOCK AT Key West in 1928, he already had a reputation for great writing. He planned to stay only a few weeks, but ended up making it his home and setting one of his books there.

Key West was not much in 1928. Its population had declined from around twenty-five thousand to twelve thousand, its economy was in a shambles, and the town was getting ready to go bankrupt. But Hemingway loved it.

The Hemingways restored a home and built the town's first swimming pool. When he arrived, the town was isolated. This gave Hemingway the opportunity to write without interruption. When a highway to the mainland opened in 1938, tourists began to arrive in droves and his home became one of the major stops on the tours.

Hemingway at his Key West home

He told friends that he once hired a man to stand in front of his house and impersonate him for the tourists. They left thinking they had talked with Hemingway. He wrote a number of articles based in the Keys and two novels, *To Have and Have Not*, which was one of his worst books, and *A*

Farewell to Arms, one of his best.

His best writing may have been an angry story about the deaths of hundreds of Civilian Conservation Corps construction workers who died during a hurricane in 1935. In the short story "The Three-Day Blow" he complained that the workers, including many World War I veterans, died needlessly because they lacked warning about the storm.

As Key West began to change in the late 1930s, Hemingway became disenchanted. He and his second wife, Pauline, remained for a dozen years until the drama of World War II unfolded in Europe and lured him again to France, where he had lived before coming to Florida. He returned to Florida several times after the war but never lived there again. He owned the house until his death in 1961.

59 — Audubon Found His True Calling in the Bird Life of Florida

BY 1820 IT WAS PRETTY CLEAR THAT JOHN JAMES AUDUBON was a failure. He failed in his first job, managing the family estate in Pennsylvania, then moved through a succession of jobs including grist-mill operator, storekeeper, counting-house worker, taxidermist, and house painter. He could do very little right.

Because he was frequently unemployed he had lots of time to walk through the woods and watch the birds. He combined his love of birds with his drawing ability and embarked on a new career. Within five years his elaborate bird drawings were fetching huge sums in Europe and the United States.

Audubon decided to venture south and search for new birds to draw. He sailed for St. Augustine but was disappointed by the lack of birds. He moved farther south, to the present site of Daytona Beach, then on to DeLeon Springs. There he stayed with plantation owner Orlando Rees (who may or may not have had the city of Orlando named for him).

Audubon made his way to the Keys, where he did some of his best work. Of

Audubon House in Key West

the 435 birds he drew for his book *The Birds of North America*, fifty-two were drawn in Florida. The house he lived in while working in Key West has been restored to its condition in the 1830s. Today his drawings fetch hundreds of thousands of dollars at auction, and the Audubon Society is named for him.

60 Two Visits from William Cullen Bryant Reveal How the State Grew

WRITER WILLIAM CULLEN BRYANT FIRST CAME TO FLORIDA in 1843, then returned thirty years later. In between, he became one of the country's best-known newspaper editors. On his second trip he wrote a series of articles describing what he saw and how the state changed. The first dispatch was from Palatka, then a thriving commercial center on the St. Johns River:

> It is thirty years since I was last in Florida. In that time several of our western states, which then lay in wilderness, have become populous and boast their large cities and intersecting railways, and count their millions where they counted their hundreds of inhabitants. East Florida still remains for the most part a forest.
>
> Thirty years ago, when I visited it, Jacksonville, on the St. John, was known only by its single orange grove just planted. It is now a thriving town of four thousand inhabitants or more, and two hotels, at this season full of guests. I have just returned from St. Augustine. . . . It has lost something of its ancient aspect: a few new houses having been built, among which are two new hotels.
>
> At present the place is suffering a northern invasion. All the hotels are crowded with guests, and every spare room in town which can be had for money is occupied. Whatever may be the fortune of the rest of East Florida, this place is likely to flourish on account of the purity of the air and the benignity of the climate, and to become the great winter watering place of the United States.
>
> In a few years, it will probably part with nearly all that is left reminding the visitor of its Spanish origin, its narrow streets, its high garden walls of shell-rock and its overhanging balconies . . . and look like any other American town in the Southern States. It will then be the resort of invalids . . . and of idlers who come back to bask in the sunshine of this softer climate and these serener skies.

Since my first visit to Florida a new branch of industry has been introduced, the credit of which is given to a lady with a Spanish name, Mrs. Olivarez. Thousands of acres in Florida are overspread with the dwarf of Palmetto, a plant which has a shaggy stem lying flat on the ground . . . while its summit is crowned with a tuft of fan-like leaves of a tough fibre. Those leaves dried and bleached in the sun and shredded into strips are formed into braids and the braids into hats and bonnets.

61 Poetry, Novels, Nonfiction: This Writer Failed at All of Them

IT IS A TOUGH CALL, BUT THE WINNER OF THE WORST Florida Writer competition is William Lee Popham, failed real estate developer, terrible poet, miserable romance novelist, and hopeless nonfiction writer. World War I had just ended and Popham was twenty when he began churning out poems titled, "Because the Violin Had a Bow" and "Kiss the Cook," and giving speeches on "Men and Swine, Women and Wine."

Popham is best forgotten for his romance novels. His first, *Love's Rainbow Dream*, had a simple plot in which a man and a woman fall in love, overcome various obstacles and live happily ever after. He named his heroines La Verne Sunbeam and Millicent Mordeaux—and the rest of the story was just as bad.

He followed up with *The Valley of Love* and *A Tramp's Love*. Then Popham tried his hand at advice books. *In the Road to Success,* Popham exhorts: "There is no higher inspiration to manhood than a pure love for a pure woman."

Inspired by vacations to the Rockies, Popham invented the travel-romance genre with *Yosemite Valley Romance, Yellowstone Park Romance, Washington Monument Romance,* and, well, you get the idea. Here's a sample of dialogue from *Yosemite Park Romance:* "I have no objections to a son-in-law like you. Dixie is yours—she is a queen—treat her as such—and may the union always be a happy one."

Not surprisingly, Popham did not get rich writing novels. He sold real estate in north Florida and was indicted for illegally promoting his wares through the mail. He went to prison and continued to spew out dreadful poems: "A Prisoner Waits" and "Dear Daddy, Please Come Home." He was released and got back into real estate and was indicted again, but acquitted this time.

Finally he abandoned Florida for California, where he died in 1953. Thus ended the career of the writer of this ringing prose: "I love every flower that nods its head o'er sparkling sands sun-crowned, moonlit and dream kissed, I love every vine that hugs the wall of home, fence or tree. . . ."

62 Frederick Remington Found Little of "His" West Among Florida's Cracker Cowboys

FREDERICK REMINGTON IS KNOWN MOSTLY FOR HIS PAINTings and sculptures of the early West with its cowboys, Indians and horses. Less well known is Remington's work in Florida.

He came to Florida in 1895 to write a story on cowboys for *Harper's Weekly*. The West he portrayed so beautifully was coming to an end. Cattle drives were replaced by railroads, the Indians were confined to reservations, and the horses were being replaced by new methods of transportation.

Remington thought he could find a bit of the old West in Florida. On his first visit he went to Arcadia and Punta Gorda to see the cowboys and the Seminole Indians. He was accompanied by Owen Wister, the author of the classic western book *The Virginian*.

Remington found cowboys "whose hanging hair and drooping hats and generally bedraggled appearance would remind you at once of the

Remington's version of a Florida cowboy

Spanish moss. . . . The only things they did which were conventional were to tie their ponies up by the head . . . . and then get drunk in about fifteen minutes."

Like the West, Florida had its share of cattle rustlers and shootings. In one classic case, a cattle rustler was found shot to death over a dead steer. A coroner's jury ruled that the steer had been killed and that the rustler died when he fell on the steer's horns.

To Remington the Florida cowboy did not measure up to the men he had encountered in the West. He found the Florida cowboys to be "slovenly, drunken, dishonest, and unromantic. They used shotguns instead of rifles or six-guns, wore farmers' shoes instead of boots and refused to carry lariats."

He also wrote an article about tarpon fishing, but advised his readers to forget tarpon fishing, sell their rods, buy a shotgun and go duck hunting. "Ducks down there are confiding birds, and a boat loaded with girls, and grub and scotch whiskey and soda can be sailed right up to them while the sportsman empties his shot-gun and fills his game bag." Remington returned several times, including a trip to cover the Spanish-American War in 1898.

63 — Ben Hur's Author Got His Chance from a Florida Political Scandal

LEW WALLACE WAS THE SON OF AN INDIANA GOVERNOR. After leaving school at age sixteen, he drifted through several jobs before becoming an attorney. He served in the Mexican War in 1846 and in the Civil War rose to the rank of lieutenant general. Then he returned to his law practice in Indiana.

But what Wallace really wanted to do was write books. He turned out one novel in 1873, *The Fair God,* about the conquest of Mexico. But he needed time to write more.

In 1876 an event occurred that gave Wallace the time he needed. Samuel Tilden was running against Rutherford Hayes for president. When all the votes were counted Tilden had 184 electoral votes, one short of the number he needed. Three states were in doubt: Louisiana, South Carolina, and Florida. If Hayes took all three, he could win.

The Republicans and Democrats sent dozens of party leaders into the three states to watch what was happening and perhaps to influence the outcome. Wallace went to Baker County where Tilden won by a wide margin amid charges that Republican voters had been intimidated. Wallace gathered statements from voters who said they had been bullied by the Democrats and had not voted. The Republican-dominated state canvassing board wanted a reason to give the election to Hayes and threw out the Baker County returns.

The Republicans won Florida and the presidency, and Wallace was appointed territorial governor of New Mexico. The job was not particularly demanding and finally gave him time to write his great novel. In 1880 *Ben Hur* was published.

James Garfield, who was elected president in 1880, liked *Ben Hur*. Thinking that Wallace might want to write a novel about Turkey, Garfield named him ambassador to Turkey. Using that experience, Wallace wrote *The Prince of India*.

AFRICAN-AMERICANS IN FLORIDA

North American Slavery Began in Spanish Florida

THE HISTORY BOOKS SAY THAT THE FIRST BLACK SLAVES CAME to Jamestown early in the 1600s. Actually, the first blacks came to Florida in 1528: Two black men accompanied the expedition of Cabeza de Vaca. It is unclear whether they were slaves or free.

Nearly all of Cabeza's expedition died, and one of the two blacks was among the few survivors who eventually reached safety in Mexico. Some black slaves were brought to Florida by Hernando de Soto in 1539, and more slaves came with an expedition to settle Pensacola in 1559. The attempts at settlement failed.

In 1565 Pedro Menéndez undertook a major expedition to establish a permanent settlement in Florida. His plan called for him to take five hundred black slaves. However, so many Spaniards wanted to make the trip that the slaves were not taken. Menéndez founded St. Augustine. The Spanish in Florida enslaved the Indians they found.

The Indians, in turn, enslaved the few Spaniards who either washed up on shore from sinking ships or became separated from their parties. In the British colonies slaves were primarily used on plantations. In Florida they built military fortifications.

When the British took control of Florida in 1763 large plantations were established and the owners began importing slaves. By the time the British gave control of Florida back to Spain in 1783 there were about six thousand whites and more than eleven thousand blacks in the territory. When the British government left, many of its subjects also fled, taking their slaves with them. When Florida became part of the United States in 1821 large plantations again flourished and slavery increased dramatically. By 1830 the state had nearly thirty-five thousand residents, nearly half of them slaves. On the eve of the Civil War there were seventy-eight-thousand whites and sixty-two thousand slaves in Florida.

The Lure of Freedom Drew Fleeing Slaves to Florida

IN THE MID-1600S, SLAVES FROM THE BRITISH COLONIES began to arrive in Spanish Florida. Their owners, primarily from Georgia and South Carolina, demanded their return. At first Spanish officials were unsure what to do.

They settled on a policy of baptizing the slaves, paying their former owners, then allowing the former slaves to work off the debt. In one case, the former slaves were put to work building the large stone fort in St. Augustine. In 1669 the Spanish government stopped paying the former owners and ruled that runaway slaves would be given protection. The Spanish policy angered the British and as word spread the number of runaway slaves soared.

In 1738 the Spanish created the first black community in North America. Known as Fort Mose, the settlement was a short distance from St. Augustine. In 1740 a British force from Georgia attacked St. Augustine, but was repulsed. An army from St. Augustine—including an all-black regiment of former slaves and their descendants from Fort Mose—staged a counterattack, but became bogged down in the Georgia swamps. Had the Spanish force successfully attacked the Americans in Georgia and freed the slaves, the history of the United States might be far different. It could have led to slave revolts in other colonies.

Fort Mose Soldiers

In 1763 control of Florida passed from Spain to Britain. That brought slavery to Florida, but the state still attracted runaway slaves. Florida was so big and sparsely settled that slaves could easily hide from their former masters. When slave owners from Georgia came looking for their slaves, slaves and Indians often banded together to repel the whites.

Spain regained control of Florida in 1783, but by the early 1800s Spain was no longer a world power and could not protect Florida. Parties from the United States conducted raids into Florida looking for runaway slaves. Former slaves often used Florida to stage raids on plantations in Georgia. They struck the plantations, then moved back into Florida and the protection of the Spanish. In 1821 the United States acquired Florida and slavery was firmly established in the new territory.

66 Illegal Slave Trade Boomed Along Florida's Coastline

IN 1808 THE UNITED STATES ORDERED A HALT TO THE importation of slaves from Africa, but the slave trade was too lucrative to be stopped by a law. According to one source more than a quarter of a million slaves were brought into the United States from 1808 until the Civil War. Many of those slaves landed along the long Florida coast.

Before Florida became part of the United States in 1821, slave ships unloaded their human cargo in Florida and the slaves were smuggled across the St. Marys River into Georgia. Amelia Island, near Fernandina, was a favorite landing spot. Some captains pretended that they had wrecked their ships on the reefs and were forced to bring the slaves ashore. Most simply landed at a secret spot where buyers were waiting.

Many of the slaves came from Cuba, where the slave trade was still legal. Not only was the largely deserted coast of Florida a perfect spot for ships to unload their illegal cargo, but state leaders did not see anything wrong with importing slaves. A Tallahassee newspaper said, "Many do not regard the importation of slaves from Cuba as a crime. They are already slaves and their change of residence to this country is undoubtedly an improvement of their condition and should not be objected to by friends of humanity."

One of the ships bringing slaves to Florida was commanded by Charles G. Cox. The captain was so sure he was safe he told a friend that "no jury in the United States would hang him for bringing negroes in the United States." Cox saw that there were huge sums to be made in importing slaves.

All he needed was a ship and some slaves. He obtained a ship, although it is not clear who owned it. Then he went into partnership with someone from Florida to finance the slave purchase.

On February 6, 1836, Cox arrived in St. Joseph, a small town on the Panhandle coast. Cox landed and told officials he was carrying oranges. Apparently a plantation owner named Joseph Croskey had already arranged to purchase the eight slaves from Cox. The slaves were seen coming ashore, and in May the U.S. Marshal went to Croskey's plantation and took the slaves into custody.

The slaves were ordered freed, but what happened to them is unknown. When Cox attempted another trip to Florida, this time landing at Pensacola, he was arrested and released on bail. There are no records to show what happened to him. The ship was seized and sold after a court battle that reached the U.S. Supreme Court.

67 An Early Leader of the NAACP Got His Start in Florida

WHEN JAMES WELDON JOHNSON GRADUATED FROM COLlege he had two choices. He could go to Harvard University and study medicine under a full scholarship, or return to his native Jacksonville, teach in an overcrowded school with few resources, and earn a small salary. Johnson chose teaching, the beginning of a life of sacrifice that would lead him to become a champion in the civil rights movement and the author of the song considered to be the civil rights anthem.

Johnson was born in Jacksonville in 1874. He graduated from Atlanta University in 1894 and then went back to Jacksonville's Stanton School for black students. At the age of twenty-three he became principal of the one-thousand-student school. Most black schools in the South taught subjects aimed at turning all graduates into vocational workers.

James Weldon Johnson

But Johnson was not satisfied with vocational courses and added a number of subjects to the curriculum including Spanish, algebra, and physics. His interests were not limited to education. He founded *The Daily American,* the first black daily in the country. It lasted just eight months but made Johnson well known.

He also began to study law, and in 1897 became the first black admitted to the Florida Bar. Another interest of Johnson's was music. He and his brother Rosamond wrote songs. In 1900 the brothers wrote *Lift Every*

Voice and Sing, which became the official song of the National Association for the Advancement of Colored People.

In 1902 he moved to New York to devote himself full-time to song writing. One song, *Under the Bamboo Tree,* was a hit, selling more than four hundred thousand copies. Four years later President Theodore Roosevelt named Johnson as consul to Puerto Cabello, Venezuela. In 1909 President William Howard Taft transferred him to the consulship in Corinto, Nicaragua. In Nicaragua he wrote a novel, *The Autobiography of an Ex-Colored Man.*

When Woodrow Wilson became President, Johnson lost his post. He returned to New York as editor of *The New York Age,* the city's leading black newspaper. Johnson became active in the NAACP and in 1920 became executive secretary.

In 1930 he left the NAACP to become a professor at Fisk University in Nashville. While teaching, he wrote several books. He was one of the nation's best-known blacks in 1938 when a train struck the car he was driving and killed him.

68 A Promising Political Career Ended in Obscurity and Bitterness

JOHN WILLIS MENARD MIGHT HAVE ENDED UP AS A MAJOR figure in the history books instead of a footnote. Menard was the first black elected to Congress and the first black to speak on the floor of Congress. From there his career went rapidly downhill.

Menard was elected to Congress as a Republican from Louisiana after the Civil War. Congress refused him admission, even though he made a moving speech pleading that he be seated. Menard returned to Louisiana, ran again for Congress, but lost a close election and moved to Florida.

As a Republican he obtained a job as a post office clerk, and later as deputy collector of internal revenue for north Florida. In 1873 Menard won a seat in the Florida house. The following year he ran for the U.S. House, but withdrew after it became clear he could not win. His campaign for Congress cost him his seat in the Florida house.

He began to criticize his fellow Republicans. When a Democrat was elected governor of Florida in 1876, Menard was named a justice of the peace. As Reconstruction ended, opportunities for blacks began to fade. Gradually, they were denied the right to vote, hold most public jobs, and seek political office.

Menard continued to hold out hope that blacks would regain those rights. He became isolated from other black leaders but he continued to court the favor of national Republican leaders. He thought he'd be named to an ambassadorship. Instead, he ended up as a watchman in the Post Office Department. He was bitter, but took the job.

Eventually, a job as inspector of customs in Key West was found for Menard. He also edited a newspaper and waited for his chance to enter politics again. The Republicans, unhappy with his support of Democratic candidates, fired him from his job.

Menard returned to Jacksonville and started another newspaper, *The Southern Leader*. His newspaper failed and Menard returned to Washington, this time to take a job in the census bureau. He tried to start a magazine, but his health was failing and in 1893 he died.

69 Plans to Help Freed Slaves Included Giving Them Florida Land

WHEN THE CIVIL WAR ENDED IN 1865, THE FEDERAL GOVernment faced the challenge of dealing with newly freed slaves. Without land of their own, blacks still would be forced to work on plantations— often those of their former masters. In Washington, Congress considered legislation to provide the former slaves with three million acres in the South, with the land coming from property abandoned during the war or seized for nonpayment of taxes after the war.

Thirty-year-old Colonel Thomas Osborn had another idea. As assistant commissioner of the Bureau of Refugees, Freedmen and Abandoned Lands, Osborn wanted to give the former slaves half of Florida. In a memo dated January 1, 1866, Osborn proposed that the government purchase all of the land south of the twenty-eighth parallel, which ran from Melbourne to Tampa, and distribute it among the freed slaves.

Osborn figured that was about 14,400 square miles of useable lands—giving each family eighty acres. The land would become a new territory governed by the former slaves. Congress passed a bill providing for three million acres, but before a specific site could be selected President Andrew Johnson vetoed the bill.

Congress passed another bill providing far less land. Under the new plan homesteads were established for former slaves throughout the South, three thousand of them in Florida. But even that legislation was vetoed and Osborn's dream of a black state died.

WHEN T. THOMAS FORTUNE WAS BORN INTO SLAVERY, IN THE Panhandle town of Marianna, his prospects did not appear very bright. Yet he became America's first black militant, a champion of black rights and a leading journalist.

The Civil War brought Fortune freedom and a job as a page in the Florida legislature. After that he worked as a printer at Jacksonville's *Daily Union* newspaper, and eventually, through his friendship with a Florida congressman, he was hired as a customs collector in Delaware. He earned enough to attend college at Howard University in Washington, then returned to Florida. When Reconstruction ended in 1877 opportunities for blacks diminished.

In 1881 he went to work on the *New York Globe,* the nation's leading black newspaper. Fortune became editor and a leading spokesman for black rights. His editorials attacked Supreme Court rulings against blacks and urged blacks to use force to resist lynchings. The newspaper failed, but Fortune started a new paper, *The Freeman,* where he was editor and owner.

He became a popular speaker, appearing throughout the country. He started the National Afro-American League, the first organization of its kind to promote civil rights. Eventually he gave up journalism to concentrate on speaking and writing. In the 1920s he returned to newspapers as editor of *The Negro World*, which he edited until his death in 1928.

T. Thomas Fortune

When he died, the dean of Howard University said, "His pen knew but one theme, the rights of man." The National Negro Press Association hailed him as the dean of black jour nalists.

Decades Later Memories of Slavery Were Still Vivid

CHARLOTTE MARTIN REMEMBERED LIFE AS A SLAVE. SHE remembered her brother being whipped to death for holding a church service without permission. Sarah Rhodes remembered that even after freedom came, the Ku Klux Klan continued to "Kill the colored people. Cut off your ears. Done everything to us."

Their words were preserved by the Federal Writers' Project, an unusual program created in the midst of the Great Depression to give work to writers. A small part of that project called for writers to travel throughout the South to interview former slaves. Because no Florida slaves left diaries, the narratives were the only extensive writings of how the slaves viewed their existence.

Some of the interviews were conducted by the black writer Zora Neale Hurston of Eatonville, whose greatness was not recognized until after her death. Most of the former slaves were already in their eighties and nineties by the time the interviews were conducted.

For many, slavery was just a dim memory. Some were afraid to speak their minds for fear of offending whites. Because the interviews took place during the hard times of the Depression, some tended to remember slavery with fondness.

In Miami, Annie Gail said, "I worked hard when I was a slave, but not as hard as I do now." Frank Berry, who had been a slave in West Florida, said, "Even in slavery we were treated better than we are now by the white people. . . . Even the white people didn't kill Negroes then as they do now."

Most remembered slavery as a hell. William Sherman remembered the dogs that were used specifically for catching runaway slaves. Sarah Brown remembered her mother being hitched to a plow on a plantation near Tampa and whipped until she died.

The narratives also give an idea of what life was like in Florida in the 19th century. The basic diet consisted of corn bread, beans, sweet potatoes, and collard greens. Coffee was too expensive, so slaves poured hot water over parched kernels of corn.

72 Trying Everything to Keep Blacks from Casting Ballots

FOR MOST OF ITS HISTORY THE STATE OF FLORIDA WENT TO extraordinary lengths to discourage blacks and poor whites from voting. Blacks were not allowed to vote until they won their freedom in 1865 at the end of the Civil War. At the end of Reconstruction in 1877, whites again attempted to deny voting rights to blacks.

In 1889 the state started a poll tax. The tax, usually only a dollar, was enough to prevent the state's poorest residents from voting. The tax was often required to be paid months before the election usually at the start of planting season when people were short of money and too busy to come to the county seat.

The state instituted the multiple ballot box, designed to eliminate illiterate voters. Voters were required to place their ballots in specific boxes, one for a Republican candidate, another for the Democrat. With a large number of candidates, the boxes were very confusing. The registrars often helped those they wanted to vote, and left others on their own.

In 1895 the legislature replaced the multiple ballot box with the Australian ballot. It was an obstacle for illiterate voters because it listed candidates by office, not party, making it impossible to vote a straight ticket. The final step to limit voting came in 1902 with the state primary system. Each county party decided who could vote.

The Democrats refused to let blacks vote in their "white" primary. Blacks could vote in the general election, but by then the choices had been made because the Republicans could not field strong candidates.

There was always opposition to the poll tax. The tax hurt the progressive candidates the most: poor voters could not vote, and organized crime often paid the poll tax for a block of voters in an effort to elect politicians partial to the criminals.

Support for the tax came from teachers because part of the poll tax money went to education. The effort to repeal the tax was led by State Senator Ernest Graham, father of United States Senator Bob Graham. He wanted to be governor, but many of his supporters could not afford the tax and he was opposed by criminals who bought votes.

In 1936 the legislature repealed the poll tax. In 1944 the U.S. Supreme Court outlawed the whites-only primary in Texas, and by 1947 blacks were allowed to vote in the Democratic primary. By 1950 about a third of the state's blacks were registered, but in many rural counties blacks were threatened when they tried to register. In Madison County only one black registered. It was not until the civil rights push of the 1960s that more than half of all blacks in Florida were registered to vote.

At the Battle of Olustee a Black Regiment Saved an Army

THE COURAGE OF THE SOLDIERS OF THE 54TH Massachusetts regiment was shown in the movie "Glory." The movie ends with the unit attacking a Confederate stronghold outside Charleston, South Carolina, and suffering tremendous losses.

But the unit's finest hour came at the Battle of Olustee in Florida the following year. In early 1864 the 54th, an all-black regiment, moved into Florida. On February seventh, troops, including the 54th, steamed toward Jacksonville. When snipers opened fire on the troop ships, the members of the 54th became the first soldiers to land at Jacksonville.

They chased the snipers away from the ships. On February 20, the 54th, along with other regiments, began moving toward Lake City in north Florida. The battle with the Confederates began the next morning. Each side had about five thousand soldiers. The 54th had five-hundred men and thirteen officers. The battle did not go well for the Union soldiers. The Union commanders committed the troops one unit at a time. By late afternoon it was clear that the Union troops were losing.

Around 4 P.M. the 54th was ordered forward. They took up a position on the left of the Union line. All around them the other Union regiments began to fall back. Soon the 54th was the only unit still holding firm. They covered the retreat of the other units, and as one witness said, "saved the army."

By 5:30 P.M. it was getting dark, but the 54th held its ground. The unit had fired twenty-thousand cartridges and was running out of ammunition. They sent for more, but what came was not the correct caliber. Finally, nearly out of ammunition and nearly alone, the 54th began to fall back.

Once they stopped and gave nine loud cheers to try to convince the Confederate soldiers that they were cheering the arrival of reinforcements. They also stopped several times to fire their guns to delay the Confederate advance.

In the fighting, eighty-six of the five-hundred men were killed or wounded. They lost much of their equipment during the battle and nearly half were without shoes. They began a 120-mile march back to Jacksonville, but although the battle was over, the 54th still had a major role to play.

The Union had suffered terrible losses. A total of fifteen-hundred soldiers were killed or wounded, and many of the wounded were loaded on a train for the trip back to Jacksonville. The train engine broke down and the men of the 54th were called upon to pull the train to the next stop.

They attached ropes to the train and helped the wounded men escape.

The final chapter of the Battle of Olustee is one of horror. Testimony before a congressional committee after the war showed that Confederates randomly killed black soldiers who had been wounded or captured during the battle. After the battle ended, the sounds of guns being fired and soldiers screaming could still be heard.

74 The End of the Civil War Meant Little to Some Florida Slaves

IN 1865 FLORIDA WAS A REMOTE PLACE. THE CIVIL WAR had raged across much of the South for four years, but barely touched Florida. So when the war ended, some plantation owners did not really believe that the loss of the Confederacy meant the end of slavery.

Union General Israel Vogdes reported in 1865 that Floridians opposed freeing their slaves. As late as August 1865, a Gainesville newspaper reported, "There are quite a number of persons who seem to hope that the next Congress will reestablish slavery. Their hopes for future happiness and prosperity are wrapped up in this idea."

Another Union general said he found former slaveholders "who still hug the ghost of slavery and hope that the State may get back into the Union with so loose guarantees upon that subject, that the institution may be revised by State laws at some future favorable opportunity."

As the plantation owners gradually accepted the end of slavery, they looked for a labor system to replace it. What they came up with were Black Codes, a set of laws designed to keep the newly freed slaves in bondage. The laws included a vagrancy act that provided stiff penalties for any black who did not have a job. The penalties usually involved sending the former slave to work on a plantation for a period of time, often the plantation where he had been a slave. Those without jobs could be forced to work on a plantation for as long as twelve months.

Another law prohibited blacks from owning guns and testifying in cases involving white defendants. General Vogdes said that blacks once again found themselves in absolute bondage. In Lake City two former slaves were convicted of stealing and fined five hundred dollars. When they could not pay the fine they were sentenced to be sold to the highest bidder. A white, convicted of killing a former slave, was fined just $225 and sentenced to one minute in prison.

Other states passed similar codes, but Florida's was the most severe. In the North the reaction to the codes was swift and angry. A majority in Congress became convinced that the Southern states needed to be punished and readmitted to the Union only after they had proven themselves worthy. In 1867 Congress placed the Southern state governments under control of the United States government. Florida's 1868 constitution repealed the codes.

BUSINESS IN THE SUNSHINE

75   Banking on Early Banks Was a Risky Proposition

TODAY, IT SEEMS AS IF THERE IS A BANK ON EVERY CORNER. But 180 years ago, it was difficult getting a bank started in Florida.

The lack of banks made it difficult to borrow money to purchase land and expand businesses. In 1821, Territorial Governor Andrew Jackson asked permission for a group of Pensacola citizens to establish a branch of the United States Bank, but no branch was established. The territorial legislature rejected a bill to establish a state bank because of widespread distrust of banks.

Banks issued their own money, and when a bank failed, it hurt not only the uninsured depositors, but anyone left holding money issued by that bank. To fill the gap, some towns began to issue paper money. The city of St. Augustine issued bills in 1824 signed by the mayor. Finally, in 1828 the territorial legislature and the governor approved a bill to establish the Bank of Florida in Tallahassee.

Four years later a charter was issued for the Central Bank of Florida, which took over the Bank of Florida, the first bank merger in the state. The legislature gave out eighteen charters by 1839, but some banks never opened and others quickly disappeared. Only three survived.

To encourage banks to open, the state agreed to back $3.9 million in bonds. The banks could sell the bonds and invest the money. The bonds would be backed by the state.

Many of those who pushed the bond scheme were promoters. A look at three of the larger banks show what often happened. One, the bank of Pensacola, invested much of its deposits in the Alabama, Florida and Georgia Railroad. When the railroad failed after building just ten miles of track, the bank also collapsed.

The Union Bank loaned money to planters who put up their plantations and slaves as collateral. Some planters inflated the value of their land, or counted their slaves more than once. The state revoked the bank's charter in 1843. The St. Augustine bank closed about the same time, a victim of poor loans. The poor record of the banks, combined with the financial panic of the 1840s, made people even more reluctant to put their faith in banks.

76 The World's First Airline Linked St. Petersburg and Tampa

IN 1913 THERE WERE TWO WAYS TO GET FROM ST. Petersburg to Tampa: a twelve-hour trip by train around the bay or a three-hour trip by boat across it to St. Petersburg. Businessman P. E. Fansler thought there had to be a better way. What if people and supplies were flown across?

In 1913, it was a revolutionary solution. Fansler purchased two clunky seaplanes, paying for them with funds from local merchants who each invested $100, and hired pilot Tony Janus. The world's first airline was born. The first flight was on New Year's Day, 1914. Three thousand people turned up on the St. Petersburg side of the bay to watch the plane take off. The city's mayor, A. C. Phiel, paid $400 for the first ticket, though fares were usually a modest $10 round-trip. Only two passengers could squeeze into the plane for the flight, which took less than thirty minutes.

Within three months, the airline had carried twelve-hundred passengers. Soon, for the first time anywhere, freight was also being flown back and forth. The company expanded and founded a school to train pilots. Fansler tried to persuade the federal government to pay him to fly mail between Tampa and St. Petersburg. He tried to get the railroad to let him fly long-distance rail passengers between the bay cities. It was too radical a concept for the government, and the railroad refused to share its passengers with an airline.

The world's first airline lasted only three months, closing down at the end of the 1914 winter tourist season. Fansler, busy with other projects, apparently did not think it was worth starting up again the following year. Janus left Tampa to join the Curtiss Aircraft Company as a flight instructor. During World War I he was sent to Russia to train pilots. He died in 1916 in a plane crash. Fansler lived for twenty-five more years, long enough to see airlines become commonplace, but he never again dabbled in aviation.

FEW PEOPLE VIEW FLORIDA AS A LAND RICH IN NATURAL resources. The early explorers came looking for gold, but went away empty handed. In recent years there have been largely unsuccessful attempts to find oil in Florida.

But Florida has been one of the leaders in two areas: phosphate, a mineral used to make fertilizer, and trees. At one time, large portions of Florida were covered with pine trees. In the early 1900s large lumber companies moved into Florida, removing the trees. There were so many trees that no one thought about conservation or replanting. The trees produced a number of products including lumber, turpentine, and rosin.

Getting the logs to market was a difficult task. There were few roads in tree-rich north Florida, and even fewer miles of railroad track. The land was often marshy or thick with underbrush. Loggers used oxen to pull the logs on carts with wheels eight feet in diameter.

Jacksonville became the state's lumber center. Ships arrived at its port to pick up lumber destined for the North. To encourage railroads to put down tracks, the state granted huge land concessions. The Pensacola and Atlantic Railroad received nearly three million acres after building a 160-mile railroad.

On the west coast, loggers found huge expanses of cypress trees, perfect for the manufacture of pencils. The trees nearly disappeared in a few years. The removal of trees was so thorough that by the 1920s the state had to import lumber from other states. Land that had once held the trees was left untended and became worthless because of soil depletion or poor drainage.

Turpentine and resin were known as naval stores. They were used in making and maintaining ships. The demand for the stores increased during times of war, then declined. Gathering turpentine was a difficult task and one of the most undesirable jobs. The state instituted a convict lease system to provide labor for the turpentine camps. The camp operators were allowed to brutalize the inmates, keeping them working from dawn to dark and providing them with little food or medical attention. Finally, after the torture murder of a convict in 1922, the state outlawed the convict leasing system.

Today, trees are still an important part of the north Florida economy, primarily for making paper, boxes and slats.

78 Gadsden County Farmers Found a Sweet Deal in Coca-Cola Stock

BACK IN 1922 THE FARMERS IN GADSDEN COUNTY HAD A very good crop. They grew lots of tobacco and the price was good. When they sold their crops, they took the money to the Quincy State Bank, where Mark Munroe had been president for thirty years.

Munroe was a conservative banker, but when the farmers brought their money this time, he urged them to invest it in stocks. It was radical for the farmers, whose idea of an investment was to buy more land or build a new barn.

Munroe wanted the farmers to take a chance on a company that produced a little-known product which one Jacksonville banker labeled "sweetened water." Munroe wanted his customers to buy stock in the Coca-Cola Company.

Munroe learned about Coca-Cola from W. C. Bradley, an Atlanta banker who served with Munroe on the board of a Georgia textile company. Bradley's bank had purchased Coca-Cola from the Atlanta druggist who invented it. Munroe liked Bradley and he figured just about everyone could afford to put down a nickel for a soft drink.

The farmers listened and bought lots of stock in Coke. In fact, they bought so much that at one time the company sent a messenger to pick up Gadsden County proxies when the Coke board held its annual meeting. Even in 1922 the stock was not cheap at eighty dollars a share. But it paid off nicely. Today that single share is worth more than 250 times the price the farmers paid, and that does not count the dividends paid over more than seventy-five years.

No one is sure of the exact total, but even today there are believed to be more than a dozen Coca-Cola millionaires left in Gadsden County. An unknown number have moved on to other cities where it is a little easier to spend their fortunes.

Gadsden County is next to the Georgia border and if it had not been for the Coca-Cola stock

Florida's first Coca-Cola bottling plant

there would not be much there except for tobacco. About sixty percent of the county's residents are black and most are poor. The Coca-Cola millionaires have contributed large amounts of money to county charities and to the renovation of old buildings.

79 Sponge Divers Harvested Riches Beneath Florida Waters

BEFORE THE TOURISTS STARTED COMING, SPONGING WAS one of Florida's largest industries. It started in Key West around 1830, when sponges were found off the coast.

The sponge divers quickly depleted the easily reached beds. By 1887 the divers were looking for a new spot. They found it at Tarpon Springs, north of Tampa. By 1890 Cheney Sponge Company had sold nearly one million dollars worth of sponges taken from Tarpon Springs.

Around 1906 Greeks began arriving to harvest sponges in Tarpon Springs. In Greece, they had learned the craft of diving and retrieving as many sponges as possible. Improved diving conditions made sponging easier and more lucrative. Soon there were nearly five hundred divers working from fifty boats in the Tarpon Springs area. In 1907 an exchange was started as a place for the divers to sell their sponges. Auctions were held twice a week.

Then the industry suffered setbacks. First, in the 1940s, a blight ruined most of the sponge beds, making it impossible for the divers to earn a living. Then artificial sponges became cheaper and replaced real sponges.

By the 1950s the industry was gone. There are still divers in Tarpon Springs, but most merely "hook" sponges from their boats. The docks and the old sponge exchange remain as monuments to one of Florida's first industries.

80 Miami Battled a Giant Utility and Came Out a Winner

IN 1932, WITH THE GREAT DEPRESSION AT ITS WORST, Miami Mayor E. G. Sewell had a question. He wanted to know why the people of his city were paying about three times as much for their electric power as people in other Florida cities? The company, Florida Power and Light, was owned by a holding company called Electric Bond & Share and American Power & Light Company and served about 115,000 customers mostly along the southeast and southwest coasts of Florida. The company also owned Miami's street car company and its water works.

When the company failed to respond, the city of Miami enacted an ordinance reducing utility rates by a third. FP&L refused to abide by the cutbacks and the city responded by refusing to pay its utility bills for streetlights. The utility stopped making tax payments and filed suit against the city.

The court overturned the city ordinance and the city appealed. In 1935 a federal court ruled in favor of the city. FP&L appealed, dragging the case out for another three years. Finally, in 1937, both sides sat down to try to reach a compromise. The talks broke off in early 1938 when FP&L charged that certain city officials were looking for bribes to settle the case. A grand jury was called and eventually four officials were indicted, including Mayor Robert L. Williams.

But the mood in the city was against the giant utility. It took the jury just eight minutes to find the four not guilty, although three of those indicted were later recalled from office. Finally the utility turned to a new president, Mac Smith, from Louisiana. He immediately ordered refunds of $3.6 million to customers.

FP&L's parent company was found to be unfit, and FP&L was split off into an independent company. Mac Smith was promoted to head the new company and the utility became one of the fastest growing in the country. The city purchased the water system, and all of the legal suits were settled.

81   A Tallahassee Storekeeper in War and Peace

GO BACK 140 YEARS AND IMAGINE YOU WERE STANDING IN William P. Slusser's hardware store on Monroe Street in Tallahassee. What you would see is a portrait in miniature of Southern life before the Civil War.

The war was about to begin, but it did not discourage the customers. Just before Christmas the store was packed with items ranging from bathtubs to toys. The bathtubs were big sellers, costing $6 apiece and beginning to appear in the finest homes. For $3.25 you could purchase a children's tub. Stoves were also popular. A small heating stove cost $10.40, and the most expensive ranges for cooking could cost as much as $55, an amount out of reach for most people. There were hobby horses for $11, a toy circus for $1.75, a tool chest for $2.25, and toy guns.

Several months later the sale of toy guns dropped and the sale of real guns increased as the war began. Soldiers purchased equipment at the store before leaving for battle. Slusser sold camping supplies, including canteens and cooking equipment, to the soldiers.

As the war progressed Slusser had difficulty getting supplies. He obtained some goods from Europe that passed through the Union blockade, but in general, his sales declined by half during the war. Prices doubled and tripled as supplies became scarce.

Before the war much of William Slusser's business was on credit. As the war dragged on, the cotton planters were unable to sell their crops and they fell behind in their payments. By the middle of 1862, credit sales stopped.

In 1864 the shelves of Slusser's hardware store were nearly empty, although Slusser himself saved enough money to continue to prosper. After the war his business returned to its former healthy levels.

82   Florida's Own Version of the Tortoise and the Hare Story

To the people working in the fields north of Jacksonville on the morning of March 1, 1901, the sight must have been unbelievable: a train going at speeds they had never seen. On that morning there was a train race from Savannah to Jacksonville. To the winner went an exclusive government contract to deliver mail to Cuba and the West Indies.

The postal service provided eight sacks of mail. Four were placed on a train belonging to railroads built by Henry Plant, which dominated much of West Florida. The others went on a train operated by Seaboard Air Line.

For the Plant system the task was more difficult. Its track went from Savannah to Waycross, Georgia, then to Jacksonville. That was 149 miles. The Seaboard route went straight along the coast and was 118 miles long. Plant had better trains with huge engines. For a dozen miles, the trains followed the same route. Plant's train ran into early trouble and had to stop. The Seaboard crew cheered and seemed to have the race won. The Plant engine could not be fixed, but the race wasn't over.

As the train crew talked about its miserable fortune, another Plant train arrived at the station, making its normal run. The mail sacks were quickly transferred and the race was on again. The delay cost an hour, but soon the Plant train was picking up steam. Along one stretch it was clocked at 120 miles per hour, easily besting the previous record of 112 mph set in 1893.

The Plant train arrived in Jacksonville to find a cheering crowd. At first the crew did not understand what the excitement was about. Certainly the Seaboard had arrived long before. But the Seaboard crew, assuming the race was over, had taken its time.

When the Seaboard crew finally did arrive in Jacksonville the conductor asked if anyone had heard from the Plant train yet. The speed of the Plant train was never equaled again in the South.

83 Now the Leading Export, Oranges Were First an Import

THINK OF ORANGES AND YOU THINK OF FLORIDA. BUT THE orange tree is not a native plant; it is an import brought by the Spanish and turned into a major crop by the British.

Nobody knows who brought the first orange seeds to Florida. It may have been Hernando de Soto or Ponce de León in the early 1500s. Whoever it was, by 1579 orange trees were growing in St. Augustine.

The Spanish liked to eat oranges but did not see them as a major cash crop. Oranges were grown in Spain, so there was no need to export oranges from Florida to Spain. When the British took control of Florida in 1763 they turned oranges into a cash crop. In 1776 two casks of juice and sixty-five thousand oranges were sent to England. The British planted new groves along the St. Johns as far south as Lake George. Unfortunately for the British, about the time the young trees began to bear fruit, the Spanish returned to power. Again, Spain showed little interest in exporting the oranges.

The trees continued to produce fruit, largely for local consumption. When the United States took control of Florida in the 1820s, the orange again increased in importance. New groves were planted and old groves restored.

By 1835 millions of Florida oranges were being shipped to the North and to Europe. At harvest time, ships anchored at Jacksonville and St. Augustine to pick up the oranges and orange juice for the trip north. Orange groves increased dramatically in value. That same year a killer frost swept through much of north Florida, killing the trees. At the time people believed an iceberg drifted down and settled off the coast of Florida.

The cold wave destroyed the orange crop and many growers moved to central Florida and started over. Killer frosts a century and a half later would destroy orange crops in those areas.

84 Phosphate Strikes Turned Florida Towns to Boom Towns

CALIFORNIA HAD A GOLD RUSH IN 1849. COLORADO FOL-
lowed with the Pike's Peak rush in 1859. In Florida, it was phosphate that
drew prospectors looking for a lucky strike in 1889.

Albertus Vogt discovered phosphate near Dunnellon on May 1, and
within days the first miners began arriving in central Florida. Phosphate,
used as a fertilizer, comes from the bones of the animals that roamed the
state millions of years ago. It is found under almost all of Florida but the
highest concentrations are in Polk, Marion and Citrus counties.

There is so much under Florida's soil that the state produces a third
of the world's phosphate. The miners who flocked here during the phosphate rush often turned quiet Southern towns into wild West frontiers. In
the phosphate town of Newberry, it was not safe to walk the streets at
night or on weekends when the miners, looking for a drink to cut the dust
in their throats, took over the town.

A few of the miners were convicts, leased by the state to the mine
owners. The work was hard, the living conditions primitive. Zora Neale
Hurston, in her book *Dust Tracks on a Road,* described the scene of men
digging for phosphate: "They go down in the phosphate mines and bring
up the wet dust of the bones of pre-historic monsters, to make rich land
in far places, so that people can eat. But, all of it is not dust. Huge ribs,
twenty feet from belly to backbone . . . shark-teeth as wide as the hand of
a working man."

A recession in 1893 ended the boom, and phosphate companies
began to merge or go under. Their work left huge scars—the giant open
pit mines—across the land. Beginning in the 1960s the phosphate industry undertook a massive project to reclaim the ground it had ravaged.

85 A Jacksonville Hotel Was the First with Electricity

IN 1883 FLORIDA'S MOST ELEGANT HOTEL WAS THE ST.
James in Jacksonville. It had everything, including something brand new:
electricity. The St. James became the first Florida building with electric
power, just one year after Thomas Edison installed his first electrical system on Pearl Street in New York . The hotel had eight outlets in the lobby
and eight outside. When hotel and railroad millionaire Henry M. Flagler
built an electric plant in Miami to serve his Royal Palm Hotel, he also ran
a line to serve the nearby depot of his Florida East Coast Railway. Those

who lived between the hotel and the depot hooked onto his system, the start of the first utility in the state.

A number of businesses, mainly hotels and ice houses, installed plants for their own use, then allowed neighbors to hook on. It meant that some people acquired electric power years before it was available to people living just a few blocks away. It also meant that electricity often came to smaller towns first.

By 1891 Lake City had an electrical system, followed by Palatka in 1894 and Jacksonville in 1895. A typical rate at the time was thirty-five cents per month per light bulb. At first service was only for a few hours per day.

As electric use grew so did the problems confronted by utilities. Many were owned by individuals who lacked the financial resources to keep up with growth. Breakdowns were common, and it was not unusual for entire cities to go without power each Sunday as the utilities shut down for routine repairs.

In 1904 Flagler built Miami's first electric plant designed to serve the general public. It burned wood and produced two hundred kilowatts of power. The first customer was a newspaper, *The Miami Metropolis.*

The St. James Hotel

By 1910 twenty-four-hour service was available in most cities. In 1925 the state's major electric corporations were formed, including Florida Power Corporation and Florida Power & Light. Florida's growth in electric use has been astounding. In 1941 the state's capacity was half a million kilowatts. In 1990 it was thirty-three million kilowatts.

86 Cape Canaveral Became the Launch Pad for our Nation's Space Program

DURING WORLD WAR II THE UNITED STATES LAUNCHED test rockets at the White Sands Proving Ground in New Mexico. The location became too confining, and the government began looking around for another site. First choice was near El Centro, California. The government's primary space launching base would have ended up there if the Mexican government had not objected.

The United States went looking again and settled on the Banana River Naval Air Station on Florida's east coast near Titusville. In 1949 President Harry Truman authorized the Air Force to develop a testing ground there, and in 1950 it was renamed Patrick Air Force Base, for Air Force Major General Mason M. Patrick.

On July 24, 1950, the first missile was launched. The first rocket was actually a combination of German and American know-how. The United States used a V-2 rocket confiscated from the Germans at the end of World War II, and a U.S. WAC corporal rocket to construct a fifty-six-foot-tall two-stage rocket.

The military operated the base until 1958, when the National Aeronautics and Space Administration was put in charge of civilian space flight and established its operations at Cape Canaveral. The government owned about seven-hundred acres at Cape Canaveral, where it operated a lighthouse. Tens of thousands of additional acres were acquired by the government and the area began to boom.

Following President John F. Kennedy's assassination in 1963, President Lyndon Johnson ordered Cape Canaveral renamed Cape Kennedy. Both the space center and the community were renamed, but residents were unhappy with the change. The community eventually took back the name Cape Canaveral. It was Ponce de León who had named it Cape Canaveral in 1513.

87 Building the Tamiami Trial Required a Special Kind of Trailblazing

UNTIL THE 1920S, GETTING FROM THE WEST COAST OF Florida to the east coast took some doing. There was a road running from Tampa to Daytona Beach but nothing south of there. There were some

Leaders of the Ft. Myers to Miami trip

old Indian trails, and it was possible to cross from Ft. Myers to Miami in less than a week, if you could battle the mosquitoes, snakes, and other wildlife.

The Indians built small shelters along the route where food could be stored to help travelers. Those who ran out could eat some of the Indian food, then replace it later at another shelter. There were large land owners in southwest Florida who believed their land holdings would increase in value if a cross-Florida road were built. So they began lobbying for construction.

There were many obstacles. The cost would be high, the road would have to run through the Everglades, and it would have to be an engineering marvel. To publicize the idea of building a road, some Ft. Myers citizens decided to stage a trail blazing of the proposed Tamiami Trial, from Tampa to Miami, in 1923. About a dozen leading southwest Florida citizens each put up part of the money, organized a caravan of one truck, seven Model T Fords, and a brand new Elcar. Only one of the vehicles was equipped with special tires. Thomas Edison and Henry Ford showed up in Ft. Myers to see the caravan off.

The driver of the Elcar was the owner of the Elcar dealership in Ft. Myers. He thought a successful crossing of the Everglades in his car would give the new model a boost. Unfortunately his car sank in the Everglades mire and shortly thereafter the Elcar dealership also sank. The truck also sank in the mire and may still be sitting there today.

The men constantly left their cars to cut a path through the brush. And at one point the remaining cars had to be pulled from the muck by tractors. The trip was supposed to take three days, but after two weeks the men were still trying to finish.

The effort began to attract national publicity because many thought the men were lost—perhaps dead. There were stories that they were captured by Indians.

Finally they emerged from the brush, exhausted and hungry. The Tamiami Trail was built and is still in use today.

88 Cigar Markers Introduced the Lector to Overcome Boredom

WHEN CIGAR MAKERS BEGAN MOVING FROM CUBA TO Florida in the second half of the 1800s they brought with them an unusual tradition, the lector. The lector was a man hired to read to the cigar makers while they rolled cigars.

Cigar making took skill, but it was tedious work. The lector reduced the boredom. Because many of the cigar workers understood little English the lector was also a link to American books and newspapers. He would translate the English works into Spanish.

The lector usually sat on a platform above the work floor so his voice could be heard throughout the large room. The lectors were chosen from the cigar workers. When the need arose for a new lector there would be a tryout and the one with the best voice would get the job.

The lectors worked in four daily shifts. One was for national news stories, another for international news, the third provided readings from novels, and the fourth from labor publications. The normal fare in Florida included translations of English newspapers, a daily reading from a novel and a heavy dose of political information.

The workers held elections to choose which novel would be read, choosing each week from among four or five. As women began entering the workforce in the 1920s there was a greater demand for romantic novels and dashing adventure stories. The lectors were paid by the workers. Usually each worker paid twenty-five cents a week. In a large factory with hundreds of workers the pay was very good. In smaller factories the lector suffered.

The lectors used the platform to advance everything from the union movement to Cuban independence, and their role became controversial. By the early 1900s cigar manufacturers began trying to eliminate the lec-

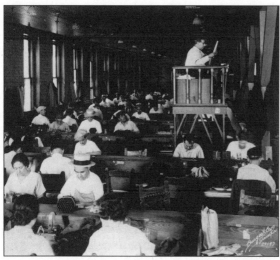

tor. He was seen as a major cause of labor unrest, often reading long passages from militant labor publications and calling on the workers to stand up to management.

Finally, in 1931, cigar manufacturers in Tampa outlawed the lectors. The workers responded by striking. The strike failed and the lectors were gone.

A lector reads to cigar makers.

89   To Pay the Bills, Florida Printed Its Own Money

THERE ARE ONE-DOLLAR BILLS, FIVE-DOLLAR BILLS AND EVEN two-dollar bills. But Florida is one of the few places to have had a three-dollar bill.

During the 1830s, when Florida was a territory, the legislature authorized the printing of $10,000 in interest-bearing notes. The notes ranged from twelve and a half cents to five dollars. The denominations included a three dollar bill. The legislature used the bills to raise money.

It was not until the Civil War that Florida began printing large amounts of money. For Florida, it was a wonderful system. The state used the money to pay its share of Confederate war taxes and for relief of soldiers' families. When the state needed money, it simply printed a batch. Money printed by the state was actually more popular than money printed by the Confederate government in Richmond, Virginia. The Confederate money was backed by the good faith of the government, which depended on how well its army was doing.

The Florida money was backed by state lands. So even if the money turned out to be worthless, people supposedly would be entitled to get land.

The first Confederate notes were printed in 1861 by a Richmond firm and were crudely done. In 1863 the state turned to a Columbia, South Carolina, firm for attractive notes in colors. As the war dragged on and paper shortages cropped up, Florida money was printed on cheaper paper or often on the back of paper that had already been used.

When it became clear the Confederacy would not win the war, rampant inflation set in. The state bills for ten cents and a quarter became worthless, and the state began printing more of the higher denomination bills. Often those larger bills were printed over the now worthless smaller bills. The early bills were each signed by the governor or treasurer, but as more money was issued other state officials began signing.

Paper money printed by Florida

In all, the state printed about $1.8 million in money. But the Fourteenth Amendment to the U.S. Constitution declared all money issued by the Confederacy and its states to be worthless. Those holding Florida money were out of luck.

A MECCA FOR TOURISTS

Early Tourists Flocked to Florida to See Ostrich Racing

WHEN YOU THINK ABOUT DISNEY WORLD OR SEA WORLD OR any of the scores of attractions in Florida, remember that it all started with ostrich racing in Jacksonville. The Ostrich Farm opened in 1892 and people paid to see the ostriches stand around, eat, and race. Jockeys, dressed just like their horseback-riding counterparts, rode the ostriches, and the birds wore silks.

In the world of animals, ostriches are probably next to camels in nastiness. Ostriches are surly and their hobby is kicking anything that gets in their way. And yet people flocked to see the birds and have their picture taken with them. The Ostrich Farm went after the tourists in a big way. At Easter there was an ostrich egg hunt and later alligators were added to the farm.

Meanwhile in St. Augustine, a couple of fellows were working on the trolley from downtown St. Augustine to the beaches. Along the route there were a number of alligators. The men captured the alligators and placed them in an abandoned beach house. To their surprise the trolley workers found tourists were willing to pay good money to see the alligators in the deserted beach house.

In 1893 the Alligator Farm opened, and has been successful ever since. As for

Ostrich racing in Jacksonville

the Ostrich Farm, it fell on hard times and merged in the 1920s with the Alligator Farm. That would make the Alligator Farm the state's longest running commercial attraction, although it is not in its original location. The abandoned beach house fell victim to erosion and the first site is now covered by the Atlantic Ocean. The Alligator Farm draws about two hundred thousand visitors a year who still get to see the ostriches.

91 One Man's Dream Became Cypress Gardens

LOTS OF PEOPLE LAUGHED WHEN DICK POPE SR. TALKED about his dream. And those who didn't laugh just sort of shook their heads. Pope grew up around Lake Wales in central Florida, then went to Chicago to become a successful advertising executive, representing such companies as Gulf Oil and Jantzen Swimwear. But he missed Florida.

He read about a man in South Carolina who had opened up his private gardens to the public and charged twenty-five-cents admission. Pope thought it would work in Florida, so he moved to Winter Haven and went to work. With the Great Depression under way it was not a very good time for opening anything.

Cypress Gardens publicity photo

The Winter Haven council gave its endorsement to the project, then withdrew support. Pope and his wife, Julie, did much of the work on the gardens themselves. They planted flowers, cut back underbrush, and dug canals. They received some financial backing from John Snively Jr., who had made his money in citrus.

After four years of backbreaking work, Cypress Gardens opened in 1936. It was one of Florida's first tourist attractions. It was hard to draw people to the small community between Orlando and Tampa, and Pope desperately needed publicity.

He turned his attraction into a giant publicity machine. Pictures of beautiful flowers began appearing in national magazines, and boat races were held to draw more attention. During the winter Pope sent pictures of women in bathing suits to newspapers in the North.

During World War II Pope served in the army while Julie carried on the business. She started the ski shows that made the attraction even more famous. At first the shows featured Julie Pope and her son and daughter. Then she added some friends and finally began hiring professionals.

Eventually Cypress Gardens expanded to 223 acres, drawing more than one million tourists a year. Pope sold out in the 1980s, but the attraction is still very much the Popes' creation.

92 The Mystery Still Remains: What Did Doc Webb Find?

WHAT DID DOC WEBB FIND ON A BEACH NEAR ST. AUGUSTINE a century ago? Webb said it was a giant octopus, the largest ever seen by man—two hundred feet across and weighing five tons. If Webb was right, it was a scientific discovery of immense proportions, a new species, giving legitimacy to stories told by sailors of an octopus that could pull a ship to the bottom of the ocean. Or it could have been a total fraud, an honest mistake, or the best fish story ever told.

The story began in December 1896. Dr. DeWitt Webb, a respected St. Augustine physician and founder of the local scientific society, was walking near the beach when some boys told him of an amazing discovery. Webb checked and saw that they were correct, but there was not much he could do with a five-ton octopus, so he went home. The next day the octopus was gone, washed out to sea by a high tide. The story might have ended there, but the next tide brought the octopus back to shore—minus its arms and a large part of its body.

This time Webb assembled four horses, six volunteers, some heavy rigging and, with great effort managed to move the corpse about forty feet, placing it on railroad ties where it would be safe from the tides. Then he had photographs taken of the creature.

The photos show something that looked like a dead elephant, although everyone agreed it was definitely not a dead elephant.

There was talk of what to do with the creature. Some suggested making it a tourist attraction. But it had a terrible odor, and the longer it was exposed to the sun the smaller it got. It would have been like putting five tons of stinking gelatin on display.

The *Florida Times Union*, writing about the discovery, quoted Webb as saying that it was an octopus but the story concluded that it was "apparently a portion of a whale." Others thought it might be a squid. Webb was pretty proud of his octopus and invited a well-known scientist, A. E. Verrill of Yale University, to inspect the find. Verrill said his school was going through a budget crisis and could not afford the trip to St. Augustine. But he asked Webb for a sample.

Verrill concluded that it was an octopus and that he should be given credit for the discovery. He named the find *Octopus giganteus verrill* and started writing about the octopus, which became known as the Florida sea monster. No sooner had Verrill published his findings in the respected *American Journal of Science* than critics began disputing them. It could not be an octopus they said, but it could have been part of a whale, or perhaps a squid.

F. A. Lucas, a curator at the Smithsonian Institution in Washington, D.C., scoffed at the octopus idea. It was, Lucas said, a whale. As criticism mounted Verrill changed his mind. His first article in *Science* was ''A Gigantic Cephalopod on the Florida Coast.'' An octopus is a type of cephalopod. His second was "The Supposed Great Octopus of Florida; Certainly Not a Cephalopod."

The Florida sea monster was forgotten until 1957 when Dr. Forrest Wood, a researcher with Marineland near St. Augustine, found some old newspaper clippings about the creature. Wood later discovered that part of the octopus had ended up at the Smithsonian Institution. Wood interested Dr. Joseph Gennaro, an anatomy professor at the University of Florida, in the case.

In 1962 Gennaro asked if he could drop by the Smithsonian and take a sample. When he got to the Smithsonian he was told he could have the entire specimen. But Gennaro was taking an airplane home and couldn't manage a three-foot-tall container. He settled for slicing off a small piece.

Later the Smithsonian lost the remainder, which is how Gennaro's small portion ended up being the only tangible proof of a whale of a tale. Gennaro's tests concluded that the sample was probably part of an octopus after all. Later Gennaro went to teach at Harvard University and New York University, taking his jar containing the remains of *giganteus* with him. From time to time his students would occasionally ask for a sample so they could run tests.

In the mid 1970s a student named Kenneth Gruber conducted amino-acid tests that also showed the sample almost certainly came from an octopus. Other researchers at the University of Chicago confirmed the tests. Still, the scientific community has not embraced the theory of the two hundred-foot octopus. *Giganteus* sank back into obscurity.

BEFORE THE TOURISTS CAME TO WATCH THE OSTRICH RAC-
ing in Jacksonville or automobile racing on Daytona Beach, and way
before Walt Disney even thought of opening a tourist attraction in
Orlando, people were paying to see Florida's original attraction, the
Fountain of Youth. By now you know the truth: There is no magical
fountain that restores youth to those who drink from its waters. And you
may also know the myth: Ponce de León discovered Florida while search-
ing for the fountain back in 1513.

Actually the Spanish explorer's connection to the fountain was, at
best, tenuous. It was just one of the many myths that have grown up
around the Fountain of Youth. But if the fountain was really in Florida,
where could it be? Some historians in the 1800s suggested that it was
actually Silver Springs near Ocala or Green Cove Springs near
Jacksonville. Others thought it was the St. Johns River. In 1934 a promoter generated tremendous publicity by claiming that the fountain was
located in Bal Harbour. In 1945 the *Sarasota Herald-Tribune* reported,
"Fountain of Youth is Discovered Near Here." It was a story based on the
claims of a real estate promoter.

In 1870 a St. Augustine real estate promoter named John Whitney
named a small spring on his property "Ponce de León Spring" and
encouraged people to call it the "Fountain of Youth." He managed to
draw a few visitors and sold them water from the stream. His primary
motive was to sell real estate.

In 1900 Loella Day McConnell and her husband, Edward
McConnell, arrived in St. Augustine from Alaska. They purchased a piece of land just outside the city gates for fourteen
thousand dol-lars. Because her property eventually

The "Fountain of Youth"

became the spot that tourists still visit today, it may be fitting that her story forms the most bizarre part of the Fountain of Youth tale.

Louella McConnell remains an elusive figure, even though she wrote an autobiography. She has been described as "a pretty woman, dark hair and eyes, slender," with a diamond set in her front tooth.

McConnell was one of the country's first women doctors, having graduated from what is now the University of Iowa in 1886. Before coming to Florida she practiced medicine in Chicago, then went to the Yukon in 1898. Canadian officials, however, refused to recognize her American medical degree and she turned to nursing.

A few months after arriving in Canada she took a job as secretary to Edward McConnell, a boat operator and hotel owner. They were married a few months later and in 1900 went to Florida. They stayed in Florida for a few months, then returned to the Yukon. In 1904 she returned to St. Augustine without her husband. There were rumors that he drowned while crossing a creek in Alaska, but in fact the couple had separated and they later divorced.

In 1908 she sailed for Spain, telling everyone she was going to look for proof that her property in St. Augustine had been the site of the Fountain of Youth discovered by Ponce de León. When she returned, she told an amazing story: A tree on her property had fallen down, revealing a stone cross fourteen feet by ten feet. The local newspaper reported that "Mrs. McConnell recently discovered a coquina cross, placed by Ponce de León to mark the spot where he found a spring of fresh water."

Buried nearby, Loella said, was a box containing a salt holder with an engraving of Christopher Columbus. She claimed it had been given to Ponce de León by Columbus as a souvenir of a voyage they had made together. She also announced that she had found a piece of parchment detailing Ponce de León's landing at St. Augustine and that it supported her claim that the mythical fountain was in her back yard. She had a local Spanish teacher translate the document, which was supposedly written by a member of the crew.

Others have told a different story. They said she had the coquina cross built, buried the evidence, then chopped down the tree. Whether she faked the event or not, McConnell was shrewd enough to know a good tourist attraction when she found one. She began selling postcards featuring the well and replicas of the salt container.

McConnell died in an automobile accident in 1923 and the property passed to Walter Fraser, who turned the Fountain of Youth into one of the state's leading tourist attractions. He was a tireless promoter who was able to generate massive publicity for his park. He also became a combative defender of the fountain's legitimacy. He used national promotion to lure tourists and threatened legal action against those who questioned the authenticity of his attraction.

In 1934 an unusual thing happened. It turned out that Fraser's land was indeed a significant historic site, though not in connection with Ponce de León. Researchers found an early Christian cemetery, and further research indicates it is probably the site of the first Spanish town in the new world. Today there is the fountain where visitors can have a drink, an Indian burial site, and a gift shop. Because it is an Indian burial site it is considered an official historic landmark. Most tourists, though, are not lured by a chance to learn about the early Indians. They come because they've heard of the myths.

94. Tourists Kept Coming Despite World War II

IN THE WINTER OF 1941 THE FLORIDA TOURISM INDUSTRY was anticipating the arrival of hundreds of thousands of tourists. The Florida economy had weathered the land bust of the mid 1920s, then struggled throughout the Great Depression of the 1930s. Finally, tourism was coming back strong. Thousands of hotels, rooming houses, roadside motels, and trailer camps were ready for the yearly influx.

Then on December 7, the Japanese bombed Pearl Harbor, and America was plunged into World War II. Immediately, people began canceling their reservations. Off the coast of Florida, German submarines began sinking oil tankers en route from Texas to the major ports on the East Coast.

The newspaper reports made it seem as though Florida beaches were a battleground. Tourism suffered another blow when horse racing was suspended because of the war. The tourist industry launched an advertising blitz to convince people that Florida beaches were safe and that taking a Florida vacation was not unpatriotic.

The Atlantic Coast Line railroad claimed that civilians needed furloughs too. Even President Franklin Roosevelt got into the act, encouraging vacations to aid the national morale. But the government also had its eye on Florida's major hotels, leasing five hundred of the largest hotels for use as barracks, hospitals, and convalescent homes.

Tourists began to come to Florida, but one of the biggest problems they faced was gasoline rationing. Once they got to Florida they had trouble getting around. There were thousands of motorists who got to Florida and then found they could not purchase gas because they were out of coupons. Hotels advertised how close they were to the beach and advertised, "No car necessary."

When the tourist season ended as spring approached, it was difficult getting a train to return up north from Florida. A black market developed in train tickets. Because of war restrictions, the railroads could not simply order more cars put on. They had to get permission from the federal government. That permission was given, and eventually the tourists were able to leave. The government also allowed horse racing to resume, and by 1944–1945 tourism was close to its pre-war levels.

95 The First Disney Investment in Florida Was a Disaster

SAY "CENTRAL FLORIDA," AND HALF THE WORLD THINKS OF Disney World. But while central Florida more than fulfilled Walt Disney's dream, it was a nightmare for his father and grandfather. Kepple Disney and his son Elias were Canadians who immigrated to the United States. They wanted to go to California but ended up in Kansas. Elias Disney was disappointed, but it was in Kansas that he met the Call family. Flora Call was about Elias's age, and he soon fell in love. When the Call family announced that they were moving to Florida in 1884, Elias and Elias's father decided to go along. The rest of the Disney family soon followed.

They settled in the small community of Akron in central Florida. Elias's relationship with Flora prospered and the couple married in Daytona Beach in 1888. For a brief time he operated the Halifax Hotel in Daytona Beach, one of the first tourist hotels in the area. Next he worked as a mailman, then purchased an eighty-acre orange grove near Paisley.

A freeze put an end to his grove and Elias Disney was left with a young son and no means to make a living. In 1889 he moved to Chicago where he became a construction worker. Later the family moved to Missouri. Walt Disney was born in 1901. By then Elias Disney had become something of a radical, attempting to organize neighboring farmers to fight the railroads and voting for the perennial Socialist presidential candidate Eugene Debs. He died in the 1930s without ever returning to Florida.

His son Walt did make it to California. And in the 1960s Walt came to central Florida, buying thousands of acres just miles from where his father's eighty-acre orange grove had failed. It is ironic that where his father's hotel failed to draw enough tourists for him to make a living, Walt Disney's legacy has filled hundreds of hotels.

96 — At One Time Unwanted, Canadians Now Find a Warm Welcome

THE NUMBERS ARE STAGGERING: EACH YEAR ONE OUT OF every fifteen Canadians visits Florida, a quarter of a million Canadians live in Florida year-round, and more are coming—at the rate of twenty thousand a year. But Canadians were not always so welcome. In the 1870s Florida workers were concerned about competition from outsiders. They lobbied the legislature, and in 1874 the state ruled that dock workers had to live in Florida six months before they could be hired.

The law meant that in order to move to Florida many Canadians would have to support themselves without employment for six months. In 1876 there was anti-Canadian violence in Pensacola when native Floridians attacked Canadians working at the port.

But gradually Florida began to seek out tourists and their money. Most Canadians come now to vacation in a winter getaway from the frozen north, but significant numbers come to retire, and many invest money and look for jobs. Some of Canada's largest companies have opened offices in Florida to serve their Canadian customers and to try to attract Floridians.

97 — Weather Is the Big Attraction, but It Can Turn Wicked

IT'S THE WEATHER THAT HAS PROVEN TO BE FLORIDA'S MAJOR drawing card, but many have found it anything but inviting.

During the summer months it rains on average every other day. Only in the middle of Africa does it rain with such frequency and vigor. Back in 1950 it rained 38.7 inches in one downburst in the Panhandle. In 1947 it rained six inches in one hour in Hialeah.

And warm? The record is 109 degrees in the Panhandle in 1931. During the summer the temperature in Florida passes the 90-degree mark on two out of three days.

Cold? Plenty of that, too. The record low for Florida is minus two degrees in Tallahassee back in 1899. That same year there were four inches of snow in north Florida, and a dusting came to central Florida. In 1973 the snow went as far south as Miami.

Tornados make an appearance ten to fifteen times a year. The fog rolls in one out of ten mornings. There have even been three Florida earthquakes. The last one was back in 1900 and it just rattled some dishes, but one never knows.

And of course there are the hurricanes. The most serious hurricane to strike the United States in modern times probably was the 1935 storm that raked Florida. The primitive measuring equipment was knocked down before the storm even got ashore, but the winds were estimated at 200 to 250 miles per hour.

The most destructive storm was Hurricane Donna in 1960. It killed thirteen people and the damage totaled three hundred million dollars. The deadliest storm was in 1928. It swept through the Keys and up to the Everglades. The death toll was estimated at two thousand. Most of the dead were migrant workers. It ranks as the third deadliest natural disaster in the nation's history.

FAITH IN FLORIDA

98   Billy Graham Came for His Health, and Found His Life's Calling

THE MAN WHO BECAME COUNSELOR TO PRESIDENTS AND preacher to the Soviets began ministry school in Tennessee. His health was poor and doctors advised him to move to Florida. In 1937 he and his family loaded up their old car and set off for Tampa.

There young Billy Graham enrolled in the Florida Bible Institute in Temple Terrace. His health improved and he plunged into his studies, ministering on street corners and in mobile home parks. In 1938 Graham was invited to be a guest minister at a small church in Bostwick, twelve miles north of Palatka. Graham had only four sermons in his repertoire. In his nervousness, he spoke so quickly that he preached all four sermons to the congregation and still had time left.

A week later, he preached at a Tampa church, this time more slowly. He also continued to preach on street corners and in jails. His ability was soon noticed and he was named assistant pastor at the Tampa Gospel Tabernacle.

His speaking style still needed work. Graham could be found preaching along the Hillsborough River to improve his technique. In 1938 Graham was asked to lead some evangelistic meetings in an East Palatka church. He spoke for three nights, then returned to Tampa convinced that he had been unable to move his audience the way the great evangelists could.

He did not want to return, but a friend insisted that he go back. To Graham's surprise, the congregation began to grow and the meetings were extended. Soon the crowds were so large they packed the small church. People stood outside to listen to Graham's preaching on loudspeakers.

He was baptized and ordained an evangelist. Graham left Florida and did not return to preach until 1949. By then he had a national reputation and drew nearly thirty-five thousand people to his meetings in Miami.

99 — A Change in Governments Meant Changes in Religion

WHEN FLORIDA BECAME PART OF THE UNITED STATES IN 1821, the state had only one religion—Catholicism. The Spanish refused to recognize other religions. In the 1500s they executed French Protestants who landed in Florida. But when the Spanish left in 1763 Protestant religions moved in.

Within a year Baptists, Episcopalians, Presbyterians, and Methodists established churches. By 1838 there were seven Episcopal parishes in Florida, enough to organize the Diocese of Florida of the Protestant Episcopal.

In 1843 the Baptists had become numerous enough to have internal disputes. The churches split over the question of missions and established separate organizations. The Methodists established their first General Conference in Florida in 1844.

The fastest-growing religious groups were the Methodist and the Baptist. The Methodists relied on traveling ministers, perfect for Florida's scattered population, as a single minister could serve small congregations in a wide area. The Baptists relied heavily on volunteer ministers, meaning they could establish churches without large expenditures.

By 1845 there were only two functioning Catholic churches, in St. Augustine and Pensacola. Meanwhile the Episcopal Diocese operated nine churches as did the Presbyterians, and the Baptists had thirty-one churches. In 1845 the Methodists conducted large camp meetings. Newspaper announcements advised "every family to provide their own meat and bread," but promised "ample provisions for those who may come from a distance."

Growing with the churches were temperance societies. Excessive drinking was a major problem in Florida. The temperance society in Apalachicola had 158 members and one local bar owner posted a sign in his window: "Choice Wines and Liquors will always be served out to those who are so unfortunate as yet to be without membership in the temperance society."

100 — Their Doctrine Was Unusual, but the Shakers Found a Welcome

IN THE YEARS AFTER THE CIVIL WAR A RELIGIOUS GROUP known as Shakers had more than six thousand members. They believed in the simple life and total celibacy. Their strict doctrine discouraged further growth and leaders began to look for a way to encourage new converts.

They decided to start a community in Florida and in 1894 purchased seven thousand acres near the Osceola County community of Narcoossee. They paid more than ninety thousand dollars for the land, with one leader complaining that land speculators had pushed up the price. The Shakers built two large cottages to keep the men and women separate and began the task of fishing and raising pineapples, bananas, oranges, and other crops. They sold their produce to local residents and the sect became an economic success.

Its membership was never more than a dozen and usually numbered less than five, with most of the members coming from other Shaker communities rather than from people joining in Florida. Entrance requirements were stiff. One applicant was sent away because he "wears finger rings and has much distaste for work," according to Shaker records.

The beginning of the end came for the community in 1911, with an incident involving a tuberculosis patient named Sadie Marchant. The woman, who had moved to the Shaker community from a sanatorium, was taken care of for six years by the Shakers as her condition worsened. Eventually, when the pain became unbearable, she asked the Shakers to end her suffering. They gave her two doses of chloroform and she died.

The police arrested Brother Gillett and Sister Sears for the mercy killing, but the Shakers had made many friends in the community and there was little interest in prosecuting them. The *Kissimmee Valley Gazette* wrote, "There is not a jury in Florida that would convict them of a greater crime than technical manslaughter. . . . Would that Osceola County had ten

thousand such people." Although the charges were dropped, the Shakers' enthusiasm for Florida had waned. In 1913 they began selling off their land.

Shakers working in Narcoossee

CRIMES AND CRIMINALS

The Case is Still Open: Florida's Oldest Unsolved Murder

THERE IS NOTHING PARTICULARLY UNUSUAL ABOUT AN unsolved murder in these times of rising crime. The killing of Lt. Guillermo Delaney is unusual: It is Florida's oldest unsolved murder.

In November 1785 Guillermo was on his way to see his girlfriend in St. Augustine. As the Spanish soldier walked down the narrow streets, he was attacked and stabbed. He stumbled to the home of his girlfriend, Catalina Morain, a seamstress.

Guillermo lived for two months before succumbing to the injuries inflicted in the attack. He was unable to provide much of a description of his attackers, other than that they wore heavy, hooded garments. Witnesses were scarce. Some people living nearby said they heard muffled cries for help but did nothing.

In an age when clocks were in short supply nobody was quite sure what time the attack occurred. Catalina Morain claimed she knew who attacked her boyfriend. She identified two soldiers, and they were jailed. But there were problems with Catalina's story. The authorities began to look further and found that Catalina had not one but several boyfriends. One of them was Francisco Moraga, known for his violent temper and jealous rages.

Francisco had what appeared to be the perfect alibi. He said he was on stage at the time of the killing, practicing his role in a play. Another actor realized that Francisco had disappeared for a time. Then Francisco admitted that he had visited Catalina before the attack that night. Catalina admitted she and Francisco had spent time alone in her room but maintained they were only friends.

Unable to prove the murder charges, the governor ordered the two imprisoned for lying to authorities. The governor sent the paperwork to Spain, where decisions on how to proceed were made. The Spanish bureaucracy took its time. In the interim some of the witnesses were transferred out of St Augustine and the case against Francisco and Catalina gradually deteriorated. They were still in jail in 1790 when Florida changed governors. There are no records to show what happened to them after that. The case remains officially unsolved.

102 New World Counterfeiters Struck First in St. Augustine

IT WAS JUST AFTER 9 P.M. WHEN THE TWO MEN ENTERED THE small grocery store in St. Augustine. A customer came in and purchased a sweet cake made in a spiral shape. The customer left two coins. A few moments later he returned to purchase another cake and left two more coins on the counter.

The clerk picked up the four coins and put them with the rest of the money. Later that night another customer came in and made a purchase. The clerk gave the customer one of the four coins in change.

As the customer was leaving he noticed that there was something strange about the coin. He turned to the clerk and said the coin was made of tin. The clerk examined all four coins and found that he had been cheated by a counterfeiter. The coins were worthless.

The clerk was considering his misfortune when a third customer arrived and asked for a sweet cake. He put two coins down, but this time the clerk examined them. He found that they were also counterfeit, grabbed the customer and took him to the city jail.

Other cases of counterfeiting were reported. In one case a boy tried to purchase some syrup. The woman selling the syrup recognized the coin as a fake, hit the boy with a stick, and took back the syrup.

But most of the coins were accepted. The coins were being passed by a number of people. Finally the man taken to the jail identified the man behind the counterfeiting.

It was Andres Escavedo, who said he had found a piece of tin and used part of it to make buttons. Then he and a friend decided to make counterfeit coins. In all, they made nine.

Escavedo said the Devil led him to crime. His friend also was arrested. The two could not afford an attorney, so the court appointed one. The two were found guilty and sentenced to a term at hard labor and they were also whipped. All of this took place in 1695 and was the first reported case of counterfeiting in the New World.

Judge Peel Became a Killer to Hide His Earlier Crimes

IF YOU HAD BEEN IN WEST PALM BEACH IN 1955 YOU WOULD have run across Judge Joseph Peel Jr. He drove a new Cadillac (his wife drove a new Lincoln), wore expensive white suits, and lived the good life. The Junior Chamber of Commerce picked him as its man of the year. He was well liked and there seemed no limit to what he might accomplish. No one thought to question how a municipal court judge making three thousand dollars a year could afford such trappings.

The answer was simple: Peel was a criminal. As a judge Peel signed warrants for police raids; for a fee, Peel and his partners in crime let the suspects know the cops were on the way. Peel made perhaps one thousand dollars a week from his share of the take.

His racket might have gone unnoticed had Peel not made a few mistakes as an attorney. In 1953 Judge Curtis Chillingworth reprimanded Peel for representing both sides in a divorce suit. In 1955 Peel failed to file the proper divorce papers, so a client inadvertently became a bigamist.

Peel worried that Chillingworth might have him disbarred for the second incident, ruining his prestigious position and his huge income. With his partners, Peel came up with a solution: Kill Chillingworth. Peel's two partners broke into the Chillingworth home, tied up the judge and his wife, and took them out to sea. The couple were weighted down and thrown overboard.

No one suspected Peel. The case was a mystery. No bodies were found, so police could not be sure the couple were dead. In 1959 Peel suddenly quit his law practice and judgeship and left town.

About that time a small-time hoodlum was found in a canal near West Palm Beach. The murder drew the attention of state investigators, who discovered a possible link to the Chillingworth disappearances. One of Peel's partners struck a deal and agreed to testify.

The judge was arrested, convicted, and sentenced to life. Peel maintained his innocence throughout twenty-two years in prison. In 1982 he was dying of cancer and was released. Just days before his death he admitted that he had been behind the murder of the judge. The most baffling mystery in West Palm Beach finally came to an end.

THE MAN WAS ONLY FORTY WHEN HE LEFT PRISON ON November 16, 1939. He headed for Florida to retire, to spend the last years of his life sitting in the sun. Al Capone, who created a one-man crime wave in Chicago in the 1920s, had been released from San Francisco's Alcatraz after serving six and a half years for income tax evasion.

Capone first came to Florida in 1928, buying a house for eighty-five thousand dollars on an island between Miami and Miami Beach. The house had been built by Clarence Busch, a member of the Anheuser-Busch family. Florida Governor Doyle Carlton announced that Capone was not welcome in the state, but Capone stayed.

While he was in jail the world had changed. The constitutional amendment outlawing the sale of liquor was repealed, ruining Capone's empire. When he came back after his prison term he was no longer feared. He had dementia caused by syphilis, which he contracted from his teen-age mistress before entering prison.

Al Capone, right, in Miami

When he was released from prison he was already dying and his mind was unstable. He forgot old friends and seemed unable to remember his time as Chicago's gangland leader. During the day his aides would move him to the dock and put a fishing pole in his hand. When photographers in boats came too near, he was hustled back into the house. He played gin rummy with his family and friends who always let him win. On January 25, 1947, Capone died of a cerebral hemorrhage. Today the guides in the sightseeing boats still point out his house, just as they did more than fifty years ago.

Florida's Coast Was Always a Smugglers' Paradise

THE DRUG SMUGGLERS WHO USE FLORIDA TO BRING IN their merchandise are just the latest to find that the state offers unique advantages. For four centuries pirates and smugglers have turned to Florida and prospered. During the Civil War Confederate smugglers brought fine goods into Florida through the Union blockade. The goods then moved throughout the South, making the smugglers wealthy.

The boom in smuggling came during the 1920s. Prohibition was the law of the land, and anyone with real liquor could make a fortune. There were a couple of popular routes: through Canada into the United States either by truck or boat, or from Cuba or Nassau to Florida.

The Canadian route drew the big-time operators because it was close to the large population centers. But hundreds of small operators found they could make their fortune in Florida. A bottle of liquor that cost four dollars in Havana could be sold in Florida for more than a hundred dollars. The run took only a few hours and a ship owner could make thousands of dollars every night.

The customers were the wealthy tourists who flocked to south Florida resorts. They had money and were willing to spend it to obtain good liquor instead of the brew cooked up by local moonshiners. As the rumrunning increased, the Coast Guard stepped up its enforcement efforts. But the smugglers had an advantage.

Their boats were built for rum-running and could travel at speeds of more than fifty miles per hour. Gradually the Coast Guard was able to buy better equipment, but not enough to stop the smuggling. Rumrunners often shot and killed federal agents.

And when the Coast Guard made arrests judges often accepted bribes and turned the smugglers loose. The Florida land bust in the mid 1920s reduced the demand for rum-running, and the demise of prohibition in 1933 brought it to an end.

A smuggling boat washed ashore

But the smugglers were ready. They moved on to drugs. Even in the early 1920s it was not unusual to find rumrunners with a large package of heroin on board.

106 When It Came to Lawyers, This Murderer Got the Best

ON DECEMBER 9, 1926, TWO FEDERAL PROHIBITION OFFICERS arrived at the home of J. Buchanan in Perry. The officers said they wanted to come in. Buchanan, a farmer in the small Panhandle community, asked the agents to wait on his front porch while he informed his ill wife.

Buchanan turned to enter the house; then the shooting started. Buchanan said that the officers would not wait for him to inform his wife and that the agents fired first. When it was all over, the two federal officers were dead.

Buchanan needed a lawyer but had little money. He turned to a young lawyer who had never tried a murder case, but who was willing to help him. That young lawyer was future United States Senator Claude Pepper.

Buchanan was convicted of one murder count and given a life sentence. The prosecutor offered a deal: If Buchanan would not appeal the first sentence the state would not prosecute the second murder. Buchanan would not accept. He rejected the deal and appealed. His sentence was upheld and at his trial he was convicted and sentenced to death.

Pepper began the long appeal process that lasted more than a dozen years. He thought his client was guilty and belonged in prison, but he opposed the electric chair. In all, Pepper received just $750 in legal fees for more than a decade of work.

Buchanan remained in prison, but he never went to the electric chair. In 1934 Pepper turned the case over to another lawyer while he made an unsuccessful attempt for the U.S. Senate. Buchanan's next three lawyers were as impressive as Pepper. Fred Cone, who sought clemency for Buchanan, was later elected governor. William Hodges became president of the Florida Senate, and Pepper's partner, Curtis Waller, became a federal judge.

The strangest twist came in 1940. Buchanan was getting on in years and read in the papers about Senator Pepper's growing interest in Social Security. Buchanan wrote to Pepper asking if he could arrange for a pension. Pepper refused, and his former client died without a pension.

107   Early Americans Schemed to Take Control of Florida

DURING THE AMERICAN REVOLUTION FLORIDA WAS A British possession. When the American colonies defeated the British, Florida returned to the Spanish. The Spanish were inept administrators, and the new United States government began a campaign to gain Florida. The first schemer was George Washington's Secretary of State, Thomas Jefferson. He hoped one hundred thousand Americans would move into Florida and make it impossible for Spain to control the territory. Not that many came, but those who did caused plenty of trouble. When Jefferson became president, he encouraged even more intrigue.

One of those who led the opposition to the Spanish was John McIntosh, who was arrested and was jailed for two years. President James Madison wanted to overthrow the Spanish in East Florida. He turned to McIntosh who had returned to Florida after being released by the Spanish.

McIntosh organized an army and captured Fernandina near Jacksonville. They created the East Florida Republic there in 1812, and McIntosh was elected president. Being president of the East Florida Republic was not enough. McIntosh and his followers marched on St. Augustine and held the town. Madison became alarmed.

The United States was already facing a war with Britain, and McIntosh's group might force a war with Spain. Madison apologized to the Spanish, and President McIntosh and his followers fled. The Spanish captured McIntosh again, but let him go after making him promise not to lead any more revolutions.

They did not have to worry. By this time McIntosh had spent his fortune on his adventures and was forced to sell his plantation to pay his debts. He lived the rest of his days quietly.

108   A Train Robber Became the "King of the Outlaws"

BY THE TIME HE TURNED THIRTY-FOUR, RUBE BURROW WAS wanted in four states. His line of work was robbing trains, a popular and rewarding pastime in the 1880s. Murder was added to the list of his crimes in 1888 when he killed a postmaster who refused to deliver a disguise the outlaw had ordered from Chicago. In 1890 Rube and his gang moved their operation to the Florida Panhandle.

Florida had remained relatively unscathed by train robbers, who had managed to become folk heroes to many and a major problem for the railroad companies. The Southern Express Company, Burrow's principal victim, had hired agents to bring Burrow and his gang to justice. The detectives followed Burrow into Florida.

As part of his plan to lie low, Burrow took a job in an isolated lumber camp and used an alias. The detectives learned that a man matching Burrow's description had been seen near the lumber camp. Detective Thomas Jackson, using a code, telegraphed his supervisor that he had found Burrow and needed help in arresting him.

The detectives set an ambush, but the outlaw learned of the trap and escaped into the woods. Six months later, Burrow was back in action. On the Florida-Alabama border he jumped aboard a train and pointed two guns at the engineer. He forced the engineer to stop the train so that the engine and freight car were on land, while the passenger cars were on a bridge. That prevented the passengers from leaving the cars to foil the robbery.

Working without any accomplices, Burrow robbed the train. The railroad was embarrassed. A single robber was not supposed to outsmart an entire railroad. The railroad intensified its search and placed a two-thousand-dollar reward on Burrow. The railroad organized a posse and followed Burrow to a house in the forest. Once again, Burrow escaped into a swamp just as the posse closed in on the house.

Burrow's luck was running out, however. He headed back toward Alabama where he was captured, not by the heavily armed posse that was chasing him, but by two farmers. He was jailed in Linden but persuaded his guards to hand him his bag, claiming it contained food. It contained a gun that Burrow used to escape.

Another posse was more effective and killed Burrow in 1890. His body was shipped back to Birmingham, where several hundred people turned out to view it. Florida's most notorious train robber, known as the "King of Outlaws," was buried by his family.

109 He Tried to Kill the President, but He Killed a Mayor Instead

GIUSEPPE ZANGARA LIVED A QUIET LIFE UNTIL THE GREAT Depression threw him out of work and made him a bitter man. Zangara, who emigrated from Italy to the United States in 1923, ended up in Miami, where he decided to express his anger by killing President Herbert Hoover; but Hoover was far away in Washington.

Mayor Cermak after shooting

Early in 1933 Franklin Roosevelt, the newly elected president, came to Miami. After Roosevelt finished a brief speech from his car, Zangara moved toward him and opened fire at point blank range. He wounded five people, but missed Roosevelt.

Within five days of the shooting Zangara had been tried and convicted of attempted murder. Then one of the five men he wounded, Chicago Mayor Anton Cermak, died. Zangara was convicted of murder.

Up until his execution Zangara not only failed to express any remorse, but said, "sorry I no kill him Roosevelt." Asked on the stand if he knew what he was doing, Zangara said, "Sure I know. I gonna kill president. I take picture of president in my pocket . . . I shoot at him. But somebody move my arm. They fools. They should have let me kill him."

Zangara's only excuse was that his stomach hurt. He suffered from chronic ulcers and said he wanted to make Roosevelt suffer. "I wanted to make it fifty-fifty since my stomach hurt. I get even with capitalists by kill the president. My stomach hurt long time."

Giuseppe Zangara

Zangara was sentenced to die in the electric chair at Raiford. Thirty-five days after the shooting, Zangara was strapped into the electric chair. He yelled at the witnesses, "Lousy capitalists . . . no pictures," as a photographer snapped his picture. Even after the hood was placed on his head he continued his shouting. Just seconds before prison officials threw the switch Zangara was heard to say, "Go ahead. Push the button." They did, and Zangara was dead at age thirty-three.

A Plot to Seize and Sell Florida
That Nearly Succeeded

HE CALLED HIMSELF GENERAL SIR GREGOR MACGREGOR, although he was not really a knight, and he had promoted himself to general. For a moment it looked as though MacGregor might become the ruler of Florida. In 1817 Florida was officially a possession of Spain, but the Spanish empire was crumbling. The Spanish maintained forts at St. Augustine, Pensacola, and Amelia Island, but everything else was up for grabs.

MacGregor, a Scot who had fought with Simon Bolivar in the liberation of Venezuela saw an opportunity. He thought he could seize Florida and then sell it to the highest bidder. His scheme almost worked.

He rounded up about 150 soldiers of varying ability and headed to Amelia Island. He also raised money from people in the United States by promising a share in his conquest. On June 29, 1817, he and his men attacked Fort San Carlos on Amelia Island. It was not much of an attack. Not a shot was fired. The commander of the fort quickly surrendered and MacGregor raised his green cross flag over the fort.

Although he had captured the fort, MacGregor had some serious problems. He was out of money to pay his army and nearly half of his soldiers deserted. To raise money he opened the port at Amelia Island to pirates. To raise more money, MacGregor and his men began attacking plantations around Amelia Island.

The Spanish at St. Augustine organized some soldiers and civilian volunteers to retake Amelia Island. Their force of three hundred men would have overwhelmed the eighty or so MacGregor followers, except for a freak accident.

As the Spanish prepared to attack, the MacGregor men were ready to surrender and began firing their muskets and artillery in the air. One of the artillery shells happened to land in the middle of the Spanish forces. The Spanish retreated in panic. But MacGregor knew the end was near and decided it was a good time to get out.

The French pirate Luis Aury arrived in port, and MacGregor sold him the fort for fifty thousand dollars. Aury set up his own little kingdom, ruled by pirates and a haven for slave smuggling. The United States became alarmed at the lawlessness and sent two hundred men to land on the island. Aury left.

MacGregor still had not given up his scheme. He became convinced that Tampa Bay would be the perfect spot to stage another coup. MacGregor sent two aides and a band of men to land near Tampa Bay while he raised money and more men. Unfortunately, his two aides landed right in the middle of the camp of General Andrew Jackson, who captured the band and executed the leaders. MacGregor gave up on Florida, but he spent much of the rest of his life trying to seize islands.

111 In a Haven for "Banditti" Dan McGritt Was the King

IN 1783, THE NUMBER ONE PROBLEM IN FLORIDA WAS CRIME. The state was under British control and it became a haven for criminals from the newly independent colonies of Georgia and the Carolinas who fled to Florida to avoid arrest. They could then commit crimes in Florida or return to Georgia for a quick crime spree before returning to Florida.

The Spanish called them "banditti," which soon became "bandits." The most notorious bandit was Dan McGritt. The British colonial government assigned a company of soldiers to track down McGritt, who was arrested and imprisoned at St. Augustine.

He would have been hanged for his crimes but fate intervened. The British were giving up control of Florida to the Spanish, and the British governor decided to leave the fate of McGritt to the new regime. In the meantime the outlaw escaped from his cell.

The new Spanish governor offered clemency to criminals who applied for a writ of safe passage out of Florida. The day after his proclamation five men applied for the pardons, but not McGritt. The British had not left, and British soldiers remained on the lookout for criminals. On July 27, 1783, the British troops spotted McGritt with several other bandits, apparently plotting to raid some plantations.

The soldiers attacked the house where the bandits were meeting. The attack killed one of the bandits, but also stopped others from applying for pardons. The bandits continued to carry out their crimes.

It was not until early in 1785 that McGritt and five of his followers were finally arrested and imprisoned. The Spanish governor sent McGritt and his two lieutenants to Havana. The Spanish agreed to release the three if they would promise not to set foot on Spanish soil again. They promised and were released. They were supposed to go to the United States, but only one did.

McGritt and a follower made their way back to Spanish Florida where they were arrested and deported. McGritt apparently settled in the Bahamas, and later in South Carolina, where he died.

FLORIDA'S GOVERNORS

A Career as a Gunrunner Led to the Governorship

NAPOLEON BROWARD IGNORED A PRESIDENT, RISKED imprisonment, and became governor of Florida. Broward was born in Florida in 1857 and for most of his life was the center of controversy.

He was appointed sheriff of Duval County, removed from office for questionable activities, then later elected. In 1895 Broward and two friends bought a boat to carry passengers and freight from Jacksonville to Nassau. There was not much demand for their service. Facing financial disaster, they decided on a new use for the ship: running guns to rebels in the Spanish colony of Cuba.

The work was dangerous. President Grover Cleveland was trying to avoid war with Spain and had ordered a policy of strict neutrality. Both U.S. and Spanish warships were placed around Cuba to keep Americans from aiding the rebels. It was dangerous work to carry guns to Cuba, but it was very profitable.

Napoleon Broward

Broward's ship made eight illegal runs. He became a hero for his activities but was indicted by the United States. It was not a popular indictment and as war with Spain approached, it was quietly dropped. Broward's main purpose had been to make money, but people saw him as a freedom fighter. After the war he lived in Key West, where he operated a salvage business.

In 1904 Broward was elected governor, primarily because of his gun-running fame. At the end of his term he ran for the U.S. Senate but was defeated. Two years later he tried again and won a Senate seat, but three months before his term was to begin he died. In 1915 a new county was created in South Florida and named for Broward.

113 Picking the State's Worst Governor Is Easy, Thanks to Catts

THERE ARE LOTS OF NOMINEES FOR THE HONORARY TITLE OF "Worst Governor of Florida," but the clear winner is Sidney J. Catts, a governor so bad it is difficult to know where to begin listing his faults. He was born in Alabama in 1863, became a lawyer, and ran for Congress. He lost and moved to Florida where he preached for a while, then became a traveling insurance salesman.

There is a story that he attended a religious conference in Tallahassee where residents of the city opened their homes to those attending. Catts ended up in the governor's mansion. He asked the governor what the rent was and was told it was provided free by the taxpayers. Catts said that sounded like a good deal and his interest in being governor was born.

In 1916 he ran for governor, a candidate viewed by the political leaders as little more than a joke. He ran on a platform of hate and found plenty of support. He was anti-black, anti-Jewish, and anti-Catholic.

His anti-Catholicism was the most extreme. He proposed a convent inspection law, convinced that nuns and priests were storing weapons to be used to overthrow the government. The election results were confusing. At first it appeared that Catts had won by a wide margin, but the courts gave the Democratic nomination to William Knott, the state comptroller, by a margin of twenty-one votes out of more than sixty-five thousand votes cast.

Catts cried foul and announced he would run as an independent. He picked up the endorsement of the Prohibition Party and to everyone's surprise won in November,

Stanley Catts, right, in his old Ford

becoming the state's only independent governor.

Once in office Catts started appointing his relatives and friends to state posts. At one time, seven of his relatives were on the state payroll, including his son, who was adjutant general. At the end of his term Catts ran for the United States Senate, but the voters had had enough of his style and he lost by a wide margin.

He returned to his home in DeFuniak Springs and opened a real estate office. Later he entered the patent medicine business and tried unsuccessfully for political comebacks in 1924 and 1928. In 1929 he was found not guilty of counterfeiting. He died in 1936.

114 Lots of Adjectives Helped Fuller Warren To Sway the Voters

At one time politicians who could spout fiery oratory were all over Florida. One of the last was Fuller Warren, who served as governor from 1949 to 1953. He was so proud of his skills he wrote a book titled *How to Win in Politics*.

Warren urged those seeking office to put as many adjectives as possible into their speeches:

> I recommend the use of many adjectives, a plethora of adjectives. Never use a lone adjective when ten can be crowded in. The goal of most orators is sound, not sense, and an array of euphonious, alliterative adjectives makes mightily for sound. For example, instead of saying an opponent is a 'mean man,' ulminate in stentorian tones, 'he is a snarling, snapping, hissing monstrosity.' And instead of saying a girl has a 'sweet voice,' intone that she has a 'soft, susurrant, satisfying accent, or la dulcet, melodious voice.' or, instead of calling a vicious man a 'cad,' really swing out and castigate him as a 'lying, libidinous, lecherous libertine.'

Warren's speaking skill served him well. He was elected to the state legislature when he was just twenty years old. He turned twenty-one before his term began, the legal minimum for serving. After a single term he entered law school and then served three terms on the Jacksonville City Council. He ran for governor in 1940 and finished a surprisingly strong third in a field of eleven.

In 1948 he won an upset victory to become governor. Warren was a character. He made headlines in 1949 when, at the age of forty-four, he married a twenty-seven-year-old Los Angeles woman. They were divorced ten years later.

He campaigned on a variety of issues, which often put him at odds with the state's leading industries. He fought for redistricting to restrict the power of the north Florida legislators and called for higher taxes on industry, instead of a sales tax. He was naive, trusting people he should not have.

Although there was no indication Warren profited personally from a series of scandals involving south Florida gamblers, he received illegal campaign financing from some shady characters. Apparently he did not know about their backgrounds. His image was damaged and after leaving office he was through in politics. He died alone in his Miami apartment in 1973.

115 Tangling with a Millionaire Was Costly for Governor Mitchell

HENRY L. MITCHELL HAD A PROMISING POLITICAL CAREER ahead of him when he was elected governor of Florida in 1892. Then he made a small mistake and ended up a political outcast. Mitchell's mistake was going along with a scheme to send Henry Flagler, the state's richest man, to jail. Flagler had made his money in oil as John D. Rockefeller's partner in Standard Oil, the world's largest oil company. Flagler also had interests in railroads and hotels.

The trouble started in Texas, where a populist governor named James S. Hogg had been elected by campaigning against the railroads and the oil companies. Hogg had promised to cut their owners down to size. His first target was Standard Oil.

Hogg claimed that the company was violating Texas antitrust laws and asked Mitchell to extradite Flagler to Texas to stand trial. Without much thought, Mitchell signed the papers, setting off one of the loudest protests the state has ever heard. After all, Flagler was pouring millions of dollars into Florida, turning it into a tourist mecca.

Mitchell began to have second thoughts about his decision. Not only was there the matter of Flagler's millions, but also a question concerning extradition law. Flagler had never been to Texas, so how could he be a fugitive from Texas? Mitchell decided to withdraw the extradition order, but this move did not quiet his critics. It simply infuriated the people who thought he had done the right thing in the first place.

When his term ended in 1897 Mitchell's political career seemed to be finished. Fortunately, he still had some support in his hometown of Tampa. The voters there elected him circuit court clerk and then county treasurer so he would have some income. He held the posts until he died in 1903.

ALBERT GILCHRIST WAS A MOST UNUSUAL FLORIDA GOVER-
nor. His background would make anyone doubt the man could ever be
elected dogcatcher, much less governor. He was born in South Carolina
in 1858. His father died in 1860. Gilchrist flunked out of West Point and
moved to Florida where he joined the Florida State Militia. He was elected to the Florida House in 1893 and served two terms before being
defeated.

The Spanish-American War gave him a chance to be a hero, but his
remarks at war's end were hardly heroic: "I killed no one, and no one
killed me." When he returned he was reelected to the Florida House and
in 1908 ran for governor. His campaign was simple: He traveled the state
handing out postcards with drawings of three monkeys. On the post cards
was the Gilchrist philosophy: The monkeys had "wisdom enough to shut
their eyes, their mouths, and their ears as to other people's business and
mind their own."

He liked the theme so much he imported eight hundred sets of porce-
lain monkeys and distributed them to voters. He failed in his goal of giving every voter a set, but the monkey idea worked and Gilchrist won. His
administration was uneventful.

Albert Gilchrist in Tallahassee

The most unusual thing about
Gilchrist came to light after he
died in 1926. He had made a
fortune in land, but had never
married and had no heirs. He
left his half-million-dollar estate
to charity and included a provision that a portion of it be used
every year to buy Halloween
candy for the children of Punta
Gorda. A bank administers the
money, which now provides ice
cream for Punta Gorda children
each Halloween.

117 Changing Election Dates Avoided Political Coattails

FLORIDA USED TO ELECT GOVERNORS THE SAME YEAR THE nation elected presidents. And Florida voters liked to vote for Democrats. There were a few exceptions: In 1928 the state went for Herbert Hoover. But it decisively returned to the Democratic column four years later.

Then, in the 1952 presidential election, things began to go sour for the Democrats. Dwight Eisenhower carried the state that year with fifty-five percent of the vote. Four years later he did even better with fifty-seven percent. The Democrats had a problem: If the Republican presidential candidate could attract so many votes, some of those voters might also vote for the Republican gubernatorial candidate.

In 1960 Richard Nixon carried the state for the Republicans, and the party's gubernatorial candidate received more than forty percent of the vote. That was twice as good as the previous GOP candidate. In 1964 the Democrats polled fifth-six percent in the gubernatorial election, the party's worst showing in nearly a century.

Worried that a losing Democratic presidential candidate might drag down the state ticket, the Democrats came up with an idea: Change the date of the gubernatorial election. Instead of the election being held in 1968 as planned, it was moved to 1966. But the scheme did not work. The Democratic Party was split by a divisive primary campaign which enabled a Republican, Claude Kirk, to be elected.

118 A Tax of Three Pennies Ended a Political Career

IN 1948 FULLER WARREN RAN FOR GOVERNOR ON TWO issues: He promised to push through legislation to keep cows off high-ways and pledged to veto any sales tax. He won the election, but before he was inaugurated, the outgoing governor, Millard Caldwell, told him a little secret: The state was broke, the surplus had been spent, and Warren would be facing a huge deficit.

Warren did manage to push through the bill to keep cows off the highways. It was a serious problem. Ranchers claimed that fencing in their property was too expensive; but many cows were be struck by cars, and often drivers and passengers were killed.

He did not have as much luck with the tax. For more than a century Florida had survived without a sales tax. But in the postwar period Florida was experiencing unprecedented growth. Warren's advisers told him the state would need an additional seventy-two million dollars over a two-year period.

The state constitution forbade deficit spending. Warren came up with a tax package that hit business. He proposed new taxes on utilities, phosphate and petroleum industries, insurance companies, banks, and loan companies.

Business hit back. They lobbied hard against the package. Warren had managed to alienate nearly every business in the state. He was not an effective administrator and could not convince the legislature to pass his tax plan. To show how desperate things were, he mortgaged his state automobile.

The legislature was not moved. Warren called a special session for September of 1949, but when the legislature met he refused to introduce another tax plan. He then left it to the legislators to come up with a solution. They decided on a sales tax.

But what about Warren's pledge not to sign a sales tax? He contended that since the sales tax did not apply to food, clothing, and medicine, it was not a general sales tax but a restricted sales tax. He signed the bill creating a three percent sales tax.

Warren had many other problems in his administration, but the sales tax brought him plenty of criticism. When merchants added up their sales they would end by saying, "And a penny for Fuller Warren." He was never elected to another political office.

POLITICS AND POLITICIANS

Florida's First Congressmen Dealt with Long-Lasting Issues

WHEN FLORIDA BECAME A STATE IN 1845 IT HAD TWO SEN-
ators and one congressman. The senators were David Levy Yulee and
James Westcott. Westcott had moved to Florida in 1830 to be secretary to
the territorial governor. He was a founder of the state's Democratic Party
and was an attorney.

Florida's only congressman was William Brockenbrough, an attorney
who moved to Florida as an adult. Brockenbrough's election was the most
controversial of the three. He appeared to have been defeated by Edward
Cabell, a Whig. Cabell had a fifty-one-vote lead, but Brockenbrough
challenged the results and was seated in Congress.

The delegation concentrated on issues similar to those confronting
the state today. The senators sought federal aid for Florida growers of
fruits and vegetables. Yulee asked that the government explore the
Everglades as part of a plan to open south Florida to development.
Brockenbrough wanted improved mail delivery, pushing for three-times-
a-month mail service along the Florida coasts, but the Postal Service
rejected his request.

All three supported measures to make cheap land available to attract
new residents. Brockenbrough wanted to sell government-owned land set
aside for use by the Navy. His plan would have reduced the price of government-owned land until it reached twenty-five cents an acre.

Westcott was elected to a four-year term, and when his term ended in
1949 he dropped out of politics and moved to New York. In 1862 he
moved to Canada. Yulee served one six-year term. His seat was taken by
Stephen Mallory, who later became the Confederate navy secretary.

Brockenbrough's tenure was even more short-lived. He served only a
year in office. In 1846 he did not seek reelection and Cabell was elected
without opposition.

120 — The Senator Fell in Love and Abandoned His Job

CHARLES JONES MOVED TO FLORIDA IN 1854 AND SERVED in local and state office before being elected to the United States Senate in 1874. He served with distinction, convincing the government to build a naval station in Pensacola and leading important committees. He was reelected in 1880, the same year his wife of nearly twenty years died. In 1884 he played a key role in the election of President Grover Cleveland.

In 1885 Jones spent his vacation in Detroit. When the Senate returned to work, Jones did not. The *Florida Times-Union* in Jacksonville reported his mysterious absence and repeated the popular gossip—that he had met a woman in Detroit and fallen in love.

The *Baltimore Sun* reported that the woman was worth two million dollars and that Jones would not leave until she agreed to marry him. Several of Jones' colleagues urged him, in vain, to return to Washington.

The *Times-Union* revealed that the woman in question was Clothide Palms and described her as a "plain looking woman of thirty-five years." Apparently she rejected Jones' advances, and his mental condition began to decline. For nearly two years he remained in Detroit, still collecting his Senate paycheck but doing no work.

In 1887 his term expired. Jones stayed on in Detroit. He was evicted from his elegant hotel, and he moved to a cheaper inn. He was in debt to a number of restaurants and became little more than a beggar, dressed in worn clothes and depending on charity to survive. In 1890 Jones was committed to a Michigan hospital and remained there until his death in 1897 at the age of sixty-three.

121 — Unable to Become President, Bryan Started a New Career in Florida

WILLIAM JENNINGS BRYAN WAS THE ONLY PERSON TO BE nominated for the presidency by a major political party three times and to have lost each time. He was known as the Great Commoner, a fighter for the little man against the wealthy giants. But this man of the people died wealthy, thanks to timely investments in Florida land and to his work as a salesman for a south Florida developer.

Bryan came to Florida in 1912 and fell in love with the state. He built a beachfront house in Miami but was called back to Washington to be Woodrow Wilson's secretary of state. A pacifist, he clashed with Wilson over United States policy toward Germany and returned to Florida.

Meanwhile George Merrick had launched Coral Gables, a development he promised would be the most beautiful in the world. Merrick hired Bryan to help push lots. Twice a day Bryan spoke to large crowds brought in by bus to see him and to look at the lots.

Bryan reportedly received one hundred thousand dollars a year for his efforts, half in land and half in cash. Even so, he denied he was wealthy. Bryan became a Florida resident and began to take part in political activities.

There was speculation that Bryan would become a candidate in Florida. He talked about running for the U. S. Senate in 1924, but backed down. That same year, he was a Florida delegate to the Democratic National Convention. He decided to run for the U. S. Senate in 1926.

In 1925 he was one of the prosecuting attorneys in the Tennessee trial of John Scopes, who was charged with teaching the theory of evolution. The trial damaged Bryan's reputation. Shortly after the trial, he died. Thousands attended his funeral in Miami, and the Great Commoner turned out to be worth more than a million dollars.

William Jennings Bryan in front of his Miami home

122 What Looked Like a Republican Victory Ended Up as a Political Loss

THINGS WERE LOOKING GREAT FOR THE REPUBLICAN PARTY in Florida in 1970. In 1966 the party had captured the governorship for the first time in the twentieth century. In 1968 the Republicans won their first U. S. Senate seat since Reconstruction by electing Ed Gurney. It looked as if the party might have a good chance of winning the other Senate seat.

Long-time Democratic Senator Spessard Holland decided to retire in 1970, and the Republicans were ready with a strong candidate, Representative Bill Cramer of St. Petersburg. The Democrats were badly divided and had no front-runner. Cramer was urged to run by President Richard Nixon, who told him, "Bill, the Senate needs you." At the same time, Nixon was trying to fill a Supreme Court vacancy. He chose G. Harold Carswell of Tallahassee, a judge on the Fifth Circuit Court of Appeals.

Almost immediately the Carswell nomination ran into trouble. He was branded as unqualified and called a racist. Carswell's nomination was rejected by the U.S. Senate by a vote of fifty-five to forty-five. Carswell wanted revenge on those who had rejected him—what better way than to return to Florida, quit the Court of Appeals, and run for the Senate?

Carswell had the backing of the state's other leading Republicans, Governor Claude Kirk and Senator Edward Gurney. Yet Republican unity quickly deteriorated. Carswell's candidacy received plenty of national publicity, but Carswell was a poor candidate. His speeches often sounded more like legal briefs than campaign oratory. In the Republican primary Cramer easily defeated Carswell, 220,553 votes to 121,281.

But the primary had consumed a great deal of money and time. The Democrats nominated State Senator Lawton Chiles of Lakeland, who proved to be a very attractive candidate. Kirk, who had clowned his way through four years in office, was very unpopular and for the reelection faced Democratic State Senator Reubin Askew.

The Republicans, who seemed so strong early in 1970, ended the year in disarray. Both Kirk and Cramer lost. Four years later the Republicans lost the other Senate seat. The Republicans again won a Senate seat in 1980 with Paula Hawkins, and the governorship in 1986 with Bob Martinez.

123 A Speech Never Given Became a Political Legend

IT HAS BECOME ONE OF THE MOST ENDURING MYTHS IN politics. The story began in 1950 when young Representative George Smathers challenged incumbent Senator Claude Pepper. Pepper had served in the U.S. Senate for fourteen years and had gradually lost touch with many of the state's voters.

The 1950 election was mean-spirited. Legend credited Smathers with delivering a speech in which everything was true, but the words were designed to make the voters think Pepper had done something wrong. Today it is clear that Smathers did not deliver any such speech.

What apparently happened was that reporters covering the campaign started making up lines for an imaginary speech. A reporter for *Time* magazine joined the campaign for a few days, heard the lines, then attributed them in his magazine to Smathers. But Smathers denied ever making the speech, and he offered a ten-thousand-dollar reward to anyone who could prove he had made the speech. No one has ever tried to claim the reward.

Here is part of the supposed speech:

> All the slime and filth and corruption you can possibly imagine are glaringly non-existent in this man's life. And even during his childhood.
>
> Let us take a quick look at that childhood. It is a known fact that, on a number of occasions, he emulated older boys at a certain playground. And this man, who poses as a paragon of virtue, exacerbated his own sister when they were both teenagers.
>
> The men in his family are likewise completely amenable to moral suasion. His uncle was a flagrant heterosexual. His sister, who has always been obsessed by sects, once worked as a proselyte outside the church. His great-aunt expired from a degenerative disease. His nephew subscribes to a phonographic magazine. His wife was a thespian before their marriage and even performed in front of paying customers. And his mother had to resign from an organization in her later years because she was an admitted sexagenarian.
>
> The facts are now clear. Do your duty.

Smathers won the election even without giving the speech. Pepper was out of politics until he returned to the House of Representatives in 1963.

124 Florida Voters Weren't Always Kind, but Claude Pepper Served for Nearly Five Decades

WHEN CLAUDE PEPPER DIED HE WAS HAILED AS A NATIONAL treasure. Little noticed was the fact that before his political career became an unqualified success he was rejected by Florida voters four times.

In 1930, after a single term in the state legislature, he was defeated for reelection. In 1934 he came close to unseating veteran U.S. Senator Park Trammell but lost in a runoff. In 1950 he lost his bid for reelection to the U.S. Senate, and in 1958 he was also defeated for the Senate.

It was the 1936 election that was the most unusual in Florida history. After losing in 1934 Pepper seemed finished in Florida politics. He set up a law practice in Tallahassee. What future could a two-time loser have?

Then in 1936 Senator Duncan Fletcher died. Politicians, including Pepper, considered running for Fletcher's seat. The leading candidates were former Governor Doyle Carlton and an Orlando judge named Charles Andrews. The deadline for registering as a candidate drew closer without a decision from Pepper. The other candidates picked up support and raised money. Four weeks after Fletcher died, Trammell died. Suddenly both Senate seats were open.

The leading candidates had already entered in the race for the Fletcher seat, and Pepper declared for Trammell's seat. He was the only candidate to declare for it. Andrews went on to win the other Senate seat. Pepper served fourteen years in the Senate before losing to George Smathers in 1950. Pepper was elected to the U.S. House of Representatives in 1962 and died in 1989 while still in Congress.

125 Florida Played a Major Role in Fixing the Presidential Vote

FLORIDA HAS PLAYED A CRUCIAL ROLE IN A PRESIDENTIAL election exactly once. It was back in 1876, when the Democrats thought they had an excellent chance of winning the presidency for the first time since 1856. Instead, through some sleight of hand, the Republicans won.

On election day, Democratic candidate Samuel Tilden led the popular vote and had 184 electoral votes, just one short of the number needed to win. Louisiana, South Carolina, and Florida had not reported their results, and it seemed clear that Tilden would win at least one state and the presidency.

The Republican candidate, Rutherford B. Hayes, was about to give up when some Republican leaders convinced him that all was not lost.

In Florida the situation was confusing. Only ten of the thirty-nine counties had reported results. Leaders of both parties sent representatives to the other counties to make sure no one tampered with the ballot boxes. A group of Republicans was traveling by train to west Florida when the train crashed. The Republican governor said it was the work of Democrats. The first count of the vote showed Hayes with a forty-three-vote lead.

The state elections board—dominated by Republicans—heard challenges to the results and after a month declared Hayes the winner. The board accepted many of the Republican challenges and ignored most of the Democratic challenges. The result was that Hayes' margin increased dramatically.

There was so much fraud on both sides that it is impossible to determine which side legitimately won, although it does appear that Tilden received more votes than Hayes. Still, Hayes might have won a really fair election. In many rural areas whites prevented black Republicans from casting ballots.

The results were sent to Washington, but the Democrats had one more trick left. They sent a second set of results—these showing a Democratic victory—to Washington. Congress ended up with two sets of results from each of the three Southern states involved in the controversy.

Republican President Ulysses Grant appointed a fifteen-member commission to come up with a winner. The commission, which was controlled by Republicans, voted eight to seven to give all three states and the election to Hayes. In return Hayes removed the last federal troops from the South. Republicans, who had gained considerable power during Reconstruction, saw their regimes collapse without the federal troops. The Democrats retook control of Florida and kept the governor's mansion until 1967.

126 Presidential Campaign for a University President

If Virginia is the Mother of Presidents, then Florida is the Third Cousin of Presidents. Not only does Florida not produce presidents, it has a tough time coming up with presidential candidates.

Reubin Askew ran for president and dropped out when it became clear he had little support. Another former governor, Claude Kirk, once ran for president and for vice president at the same time, and former Senator Claude Pepper ran for president for two days in 1948.

And then there is the strange noncandidacy of Albert Murphree in 1924. Murphree was the president of the University of Florida and had absolutely no interest in any political office. Then William Jennings Bryan came along. Bryan had been a three-time Democratic nominee for president and came up short in two other tries for the nomination. He moved to Florida and went into the real estate business in Miami. He continued to be a force in national politics, making speeches around the country. While in Gainesville he met Murphree and was immediately impressed.

In 1909 Murphree had become president of the University of Florida. The university was only four years old and not doing very well when he arrived. He increased enrollment, improved academic standards, and created a number of new schools.

In January 1924 Bryan surprised everyone, including Murphree, by announcing that he would back the university president for the Democratic presidential nomination. Reporters flocked to interview

Murphree, who insisted that he did not want to be president.

The leading candidate, John Davis, advocated the repeal of Prohibition. To Democrats, who favored keeping the nation dry, Murphree looked like a good candidate. He won newspaper endorsements and support from throughout the country. Murphree said, "Nobody expects a Southern man to be nominated president, much less a Florida man."

Bryan was out of touch with the Democratic Party. When he rose to speak on behalf of Murphree at the convention, he was greeted with boos and catcalls. Davis won the nomination and was routed by President Calvin Coolidge in November.

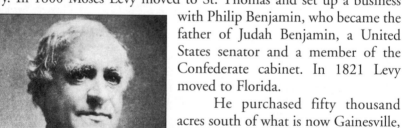

127 The Senator's Father Dreamed of a Jewish Refuge in Florida

ONE OF FLORIDA'S BIGGEST LAND BOOMS TOOK PLACE between 1819 and 1821 as the territory changed hands from Spain to the United States. Spain had granted huge tracts of land to its citizens, such as the 289,000-acre Arredondo grant in the area around what is now Gainesville. The Spanish landholders frequently decided to sell rather than risk losing their grants under American law.

The Arredondo grant attracted Moses Levy of St. Thomas in the Virgin Islands. He was a lumber merchant and businessman whose ancestors were expelled from Spain in 1492 along with other Jews. They then fled to Morocco where the family name became Yulee.

When the family moved to Gibraltar the name was transformed to Levy. In 1800 Moses Levy moved to St. Thomas and set up a business with Philip Benjamin, who became the father of Judah Benjamin, a United States senator and a member of the Confederate cabinet. In 1821 Levy moved to Florida.

David Levy Yulee

He purchased fifty thousand acres south of what is now Gainesville, where he hoped to establish a plantation and a colony for Jewish families. Levy took out advertisements in European newspapers to publicize his project. He named his plantation New Pilgrimage. The first settlers for his community arrived in 1822 from northern states and set about building houses and a stable. Levy also expanded his land holdings. He purchased land in what is now Tampa and on the St. Johns River. But his settlement at New Pilgrimage was a failure. The colonists either died of disease or moved back north.

Moses Levy's son David was more of a success. He was one of the founders of Florida as a state. From 1841 to 1845 he served as a territorial delegate and played a key role in pushing for statehood. When Florida became a state in 1845, David Levy became one of Florida's first U. S. senators. At the same time Levy petitioned the legislature to change his name back to the original family name of Yulee. That is why Florida has a county named Levy and a town named Yulee, both named for the same man.

128 Some Have Found Trouble Here, but Presidents Keep On Coming

PRESIDENTS KEEP COMING TO FLORIDA, ATTRACTED BY THE fine weather or the large number of voters. But for many the state has held plenty of bad memories. Consider the bad luck of Franklin Roosevelt. He once had a yacht anchored in south Florida. Then a hurricane picked it up and carried it inland several miles before depositing it in a marsh. Unable to move it, Roosevelt put a "for sale" sign on it and told people it was a hunting lodge. It did not sell. When Roosevelt came to Miami shortly before his 1933 inauguration Guiseppe Zangara tried to assassinate him. Instead, one bullet killed Chicago Mayor Anton Cermak.

Andrew Jackson first came to Florida to fight Indians in 1818. He was so successful that in 1821 he was appointed as the first territorial governor. President James Monroe said, "I have full confidence that your appointment will be immediately and most beneficially felt. Smugglers and slave traders will hide their heads; pirates will disappear, and

Spiro Agnew and Richard Nixon in Miami Beach

Seminoles cease to give trouble." Jackson set up the new government in Pensacola, but he hated Pensacola and Florida, and before the year was out he quit and went back to Tennessee. For the rest of his life, he never had anything good to say about Florida and he never came back.

Zachary Taylor did find fame in Florida. He and his eight hundred men defeated four hundred Indians in 1838. The battle all but ended Indian resistance in Florida and helped elect Taylor to the presidency in 1848. He died in office.

Ulysses Grant came to Florida after leaving office in 1881 to turn the first shovel of dirt for a railroad between Sanford and Orlando. The trip encouraged Grant to enter the railroad business—where he promptly lost his fortune and almost went to prison for fraud.

The first president to come to Florida while in office was Chester A. Arthur in 1883. He came for the fishing in Kissimmee and to see friends in Maitland. But he didn't come to see the voters. "I am here for rest, not for public display," he told an aide. When he left Maitland for the return trip to Washington someone suggested that the train stop in downtown Orlando so that Arthur could say hello to the folks. "I say that we shall not stop at Orlando," Arthur snapped.

When William McKinley visited Tallahassee in 1899 the crowds were so great that his wife fainted. He never came back.

When William Howard Taft came through around 1911 his train was supposed to stop—but somebody forgot. The community of Taft is named for the spot where Taft's train did not stop. About fifteen years later, Calvin Coolidge was also supposed to stop in Orlando, but again somebody forgot. By the time Coolidge remembered he was out of town and all anybody saw was the president waving from the back of a train.

After Warren G. Harding was elected in 1920 he was lured to Miami Beach by land developers for a few rounds of golf. To make sure the developers got the maximum publicity they had Harding use an elephant as his caddy. He was supposed to come to Sarasota in 1923 to help promote the area but died before making the trip.

Three presidents had second homes in Florida. Harry Truman used a house on the grounds of the U.S. Navy base in Key West as a second home. He called it "The Little White House." Truman also came to Orlando in 1949, drawing nearly a hundred thousand people for the dedication of a causeway between Orlando and Winter Park. John Kennedy's father owned an estate in Palm Beach, and Kennedy was a frequent visitor there. He spent the weekend in Palm Beach before his ill-fated trip to Dallas in 1963.

But no president has been closer to Florida than Richard Nixon. He started coming to the state in 1946 to visit friends in Miami. When he became president he purchased a home in Key Biscayne. He was vacationing in Key Biscayne in 1972 when a group of men broke into the Democratic National Committee headquarters in Washington. An aide called what later became the Watergate scandal a "third-rate burglary." Two years later Nixon was in Orlando when he uttered his famous words, "I am not a crook."

129   Women Finally Gained the Vote, but No Thanks to Florida

MORE THAN A CENTURY AGO ELLA C. CHAMBERLAIN TRAV-eled from her home in Tampa to Des Moines, Iowa, for a convention of women attempting to secure the right to vote. The next year she formed the Florida Woman Suffrage Association. The campaign did not go well, and the group disbanded in 1897 when Chamberlain left the state.

It was not until 1912 that another organization—the Florida Equal Franchise League—was created to campaign for the vote for women. The league had its headquarters in Jacksonville. The same year, a group of women tried to vote in Florida for the first time. A municipal bond election was being held in Orlando. The mayor announced that all property owners could vote. Because the mayor's announcement did not say "male" property owners, some women tried to register. They were turned away.

In 1913 women in Volusia County formed an organization to push for voting rights; within months another group was formed in Orlando. The state's suffrage groups met in Orlando late in 1913 to form the Florida Equal Suffrage Association. The membership varied from seven hundred to eight hundred; the larger chapters were in Jacksonville, Ocala, Pensacola, and Miami. While most association members limited their activities to education and polite lobbying, Mary Nolan of Jacksonville went to Washington to picket the White House. The seventy-three-year-old woman was arrested and spent six days in jail.

The Florida legislature considered approving a constitutional amendment to give women the right to vote, but the bill died with little debate. State Representative John M. Gornto of Lafayette County told the legislature that giving the vote to women would "bring on marital unhappiness, divorces, and a disruptive domestic condition." The legislature continued to reject the amendment while Congress approved an amendment to the Constitution giving women the right to vote in federal elections. The amendment was approved in 1920 by the required number of states and became law, even though Florida voted against it.

130   Like Suffrage Before It, ERA Met Defeat in Florida

WHEN THE U.S. CONGRESS PASSED THE EQUAL RIGHTS Amendment to the Constitution in 1972 and sent it to the states for ratification, it looked like a sure thing. States lined up to approve the amendment. In Florida, the house quickly gave its overwhelming approval. But the session was coming to an end, and the senate put off consideration until the next year.

It did not seem to matter. What difference could a year make? Florida, which had failed to ratify the amendment giving women the right to vote, would certainly pass the ERA. As it turned out, it made a huge difference.

After the state senate failed to pass the bill, opposition began to develop. Conservative groups claimed that the amendment would actually hurt women, lead to unisex bathrooms, and force women to take part in combat. Legislators caved in as they began receiving thousands of letters demanding that they vote against the bill. Many of the letters were not even from Florida.

By the time the 1973 session opened, the opposition was fierce. The house, which had passed the amendment by nearly ninety votes in 1972, rejected it by a ten-vote margin the following year. The senate did not consider the bill that year.

In 1974 the senate considered the matter first. State Senator Dempsey Barron was the dominant force in the senate, and he was opposed to the amendment. He worked behind the scenes for its defeat. It failed to pass by a vote of twenty-one to nineteen.

In 1975 the amendment came up in both the house and senate. In the house it passed by a three-vote margin, but in the senate the amendment had lost ground and it failed by four votes. There was no ERA vote in 1976.

In 1977 the house was ready once again to approve the measure. Florida had become a crucial state for ERA. The amendment had been approved by thirty-five states, just three short of the number needed for approval. There was intense pressure on the senate to pass the amendment but it was defeated by two votes. The amendment was not considered in 1978.

Again in 1979 it was considered by both the house and the senate. The house again passed the measure but the senate was deeply divided. The result was familiar, a loss by two votes. It was the last time both houses of the legislature voted on the amendment. In 1982 the senate again defeated the amendment, and the house never voted on it. Then time ran out on the Equal Rights Amendment.

131 Our Sixth President Was the First to Fight for Florida's Environment

IN 1827 NO ONE WAS PARTICULARLY CONCERNED ABOUT protecting Florida's environment. That is when President John Quincy Adams became Florida's first environmentalist. In the early 1800s huge live oak trees covered much of north Florida. Then people began moving into north Florida and discovered that the oak trees were more valuable than any crop. The lumber was highly prized by shipbuilders, and the forests were quickly chopped away.

In 1827 Samuel Southard, the secretary of the navy, told Congress the forests were disappearing at an alarming rate. Southard was concerned because the oaks were vital to building a navy. The government moved to protect the oak trees by limiting land sales.

Still, the chopping continued. Groups of men would move onto government-owned land and quickly strip a forest bare. Naturalist John J. Audubon called the cutters "Live-Oakers." Their activities spurred President John Quincy Adams to step in.

Adams was a lover of trees and decided something had to be done to save the oaks. Congress passed Adams' bill to establish a sixty-thousand-acre reservation near Pensacola to protect the trees and grow new ones.

Judge Henry Brackenridge was named to supervise the reservation. It was a short-lived success. In the election of 1828 Adams was defeated by Andrew Jackson. The new president was no lover of trees and had no use for conservation. Jackson aides accused the Adams administration of making illegal profits in the buying of reservation land, even though a government investigation found no wrongdoing.

Brackenridge tired of the controversy and moved back to Pennsylvania. Congress did pass a law in 1831 to ban the cutting of trees on U.S. land, but it was impossible to enforce in lightly populated Florida. The government lost interest in the oak reservation. Soon the Live-Oakers came back and began chopping down the trees. There is a town in north Florida named Live Oak, but only a fraction of the region's once-great oaks remain.

132 Low State Taxes Were Meant to Lure Wealthy Residents

FLORIDA IS NOT KNOWN JUST FOR ITS SUNSHINE AND ATTRACtions. It also has a reputation for low taxes. Florida ranks in the bottom third out of fifty states in tax collections. The low tax rate is not a fluke. Until 1932 Florida had only a handful of taxes, generating a small amount of money. There were taxes on gasoline, car registration, and property. Then the legislature gave the property tax back to local governments and added taxes on pari-mutuel betting. In 1935 the state added taxes on beer, wine, and liquor.

Florida's tax structure was designed to lure wealthy northerners to Florida. The idea was to make taxes so low that northerners would find it worth their while to move to Florida to save money. There cannot be an income tax in Florida unless the constitution is changed by the voters, and the inheritance tax is the most attractive in the country.

That means the state has to look in lots of places for its money. In 1943 the state passed its first cigarette tax—three cents per pack. In 1949 the state passed its broadest tax, a three percent sales tax. The governor who proposed it, Fuller Warren, never won another election. The sales tax was raised to four percent in 1968 and to five percent in 1982. The tax is now six percent with conties having the option of adding a penny.

The sales tax makes up about two thirds of the state's income. The corporate income tax takes in about nine percent and the beverage tax produces seven percent. Documentary stamps on such things as real-estate transactions kick in four percent. All the other taxes account for the rest.

133 Presidential Timber Hasn't Put Down Roots in Florida Yet

FLORIDA IS THE LARGEST STATE IN THE UNION NEVER TO HAVE a native serve as president. But it does have the dubious distinction of having the shortest presidential campaign. The year was 1948 and President Harry Truman was seeking his party's nomination, but Truman was very unpopular—so unpopular that one of the slogans at the time was, "To Err Is Truman."

Democrats were concerned that Truman would go down to a smashing defeat and pull other Democrats down with him. His opponents within the party began casting around for another candidate. They decided that the only candidate who could save the party was Dwight Eisenhower, the former allied commander in World War II, who had become president of Columbia University. Eisenhower told the Democrats he was not interested, but they kept pushing.

Just before the convention opened in July, Florida Senator Claude Pepper announced that he would nominate Eisenhower, even though the general did not want to be nominated. That brought another statement from Eisenhower, this one more direct and angry. He would not run, he said, and wanted efforts on his behalf to stop immediately.

At this point Pepper mentioned that he was available if anyone wanted to nominate him for president. Nobody did. Many of the unhappy Democrats turned to Truman, but a few held out. They hoped to convince Supreme Court Justice William Douglas to run.

Douglas also said no, and the anti-Truman forces had run out of possibilities. Again Pepper declared his willingness to run, and nearly everyone yawned. But Pepper would not be stopped. He declared his candidacy in what the *New York Times* called the funniest moment of the convention. He indicated that he thought he would get hundreds of delegates, but it turned out he had just six and a half, including himself.

His candidacy became a joke, and a day and a half after he announced, Pepper said that he was withdrawing. Truman was nominated but never forgot that Pepper had tried to deny him the nomination. When Pepper ran for reelection for the Senate in 1950, Truman secretly encouraged his primary opponent, George Smathers. Pepper lost in a bitter race.

134 The Johns Committee Ruined Lives, but Its Files Were Kept Secret

EVERY STATE HAS ITS LITTLE SECRETS—THE KINDS OF THINGS nobody puts on billboards to lure tourists or brags about to attract new industry. In Florida one of those secrets is the Johns Committee. The Johns Committee, named for Charley Johns, a one-time acting governor, was officially known as the Florida Legislative Investigation Committee.

The joint house and senate committee was formed in the 1950s and lasted into the 1960s. Its purpose was never quite clear, but its impact was. The committee conducted a campaign of terror, seeking to identify people who supported integrating state universities. The committee was also looking for people it thought were Communists or homosexuals.

The goal of the committee was to destroy careers of anyone who opposed it or anyone who worked for a state university and supported civil rights. While it existed, it leaked information to newspapers to di credit its opponents and others it wanted to harm. It used executive sessions to protect the testimony it obtained, then leaked the information it chose. The committee was opposed by LeRoy Collins, who had defeated Johns for the governorship.

The records of the Johns Committee were stored in boxes in Tallahassee after the committee folded. In 1990 James Schnur, a graduate student at the University of South Florida, began doing research on the committee. That school had been particularly hard hit by the work of the Johns

Johns committee meeting in Tallahassee

Committee. Schnur was working on a paper about the committee. His paper won an award, and Schnur wanted to find out more.

To do that he needed to see the records of the Johns Committee. The records had remained closed for nearly thirty years, and most of those involved, including Johns, were dead. There seemed to be no reason to protect Johns or his fellow committee members. Those who were attacked by Johns already had been identified through leaks.

Schnur wrote to Senate President Gwen Margolis asking that she release the committee records. Margolis had the power to do that and show the truth about how Johns and his committee operated. Other senate presidents had rejected such requests, but Margolis went a huge step farther. She ruled that no one could see the records until December 31, 2028. Why 2028? Margolis decided that since census records are kept secret for seventy-two years the Johns Committee records also should be secret for that long. The Margolis decision did not stand, and the papers were later opened.

135 Florida's 1931 Legislature May Have Hit an All-Time Low

EACH YEAR THE FLORIDA LEGISLATURE PROVIDES NEW hijinks: mistaken votes, bills passed in error, and the kind of general confusion that often takes months and special sessions to correct. But the 1931 session is special to Allen Morris, historian of the Florida House of Representatives. It was a session with a little of everything.

The legislature met as the Great Depression took hold in Florida. Banks were failing, money was scarce, and nobody knew what to expect. The legislature responded with its most unusual session:

The session lasted one hundred days, the longest to that time.

In an effort to provide jobs for veterans, the legislature passed a bill to allow any veteran to become a certified public accountant without any training or education. The governor vetoed the bill. After a spending bill passed the house, a clerk apparently added an amendment without telling anyone.

The legislature passed a bill to regulate barbers but rejected an amendment to require truth-in-labeling on hair tonics. For the first time, the senate voted to allow its members to remove their coats during the session. A Jacksonville representative filibustered for three days, still a record.

The legislature had to reduce overall state spending because of the Depression, but managed to raise members' salaries from $5,400 to $6,000 a year.

The legislature passed a bill establishing pari-mutuel horse racing. The governor vetoed the bill, but the legislature overrode the veto. There were rumors that more than one hundred thousand dollars had been paid to legislators to vote for racing.

Florida's voters apparently didn't think much of the session. A record twenty-six out of ninety-five house members were defeated in reelection bids, and another thirty-one did not seek reelection.

136 Trying to Pick Second-Choice Nominees Led to Confusion at the Polls

BACK AROUND THE TURN OF THE CENTURY THERE WAS ONLY one real political party in Florida—the Democrats. A candidate who won the Democratic primary won the election. In a large field of primary candidates, someone could win with a small percentage of the vote if everyone else got less. So Florida and seven other Southern states created the runoff primary. If no candidate got more than fifty percent of the vote, there would be a runoff.

That worked fine until 1913 when Florida figured it cost too much money to hold a second primary. The state came up with the idea of having second-choice votes. There would be one primary in which folks would vote for their favorite candidate. Then they would also vote for their second choice. If no candidate got more than fifty percent, the second choice votes would be added in.

The new method turned the 1916 primary into a disaster. Sidney J. Catts received $30,000 first place votes while his opponent William V. Knott got 24,756 votes. But Catts did not have fifty percent. Knott received 8,674 second choice votes while Catts had 3,351. Knott claimed victory by a handful of votes, and the courts upheld him. But Catts cried foul and ran as an independent, defeating Knott in the general election and becoming governor. The second choice votes remained through the 1932 election, but never again played a major role in determining the winner.

In 1932 the state returned to the runoff primary. Since then, the leader in six firts-round gubernatorial primaries lost in the second election. What would have happened if there had only been one primary? Bob Graham would not have been elected governor, Reubin Askew would not have been governor, and Lawton Chiles would not have been elected to the United States Senate.

BAD NEWS

Going to the Dogs Proved to Be a Major Mistake

FROM THE START, IT WAS A TERRIBLE IDEA. BEGINNING IN 1835 the federal government tried to round up thousands of Seminole Indians who lived in Florida and move them to Oklahoma. Some Indians went but many resisted, hiding in the woods and swamps. Federal troops had difficulty finding them and were often the targets of surprise attacks.

Finally some Florida folks came up with the idea of buying bloodhounds to find the Indians. There were no bloodhounds in Florida, and the nearest dogs were in Cuba.

Territorial officials ordered some dogs from Cuba for the high cost of $151.72 each. Questions about the cost were raised in Washington; then people began to wonder how bloodhounds could tell the Indians from non-Indians when they went out sniffing.

There was another problem: The dogs did not understand English. They had been trained in Cuba and understood only Spanish commands. The next step was to hire their Spanish trainers. The dogs also had to have a rather expensive diet: the meat from tender calves. The dogs were eating better than the soldiers. They also were traveling better than the soldiers. The dogs were not especially fond of walking, so they were placed on horses and the soldiers walked alongside

In the end they never did sniff out any Indians. What they did find were lots of soldiers. Once when they were turned loose to hunt Indians they ended up sniffing out General Zachary Taylor, the commander of American troops in Florida and future president.

The experiment ended quickly. The Florida legislature tried to bill Taylor $2,429.52 for the dogs, but he said that because they had not done any work he would not pay. The bill was never paid.

---

138 | The Dream of a Canal Endured for Four Hundred Years

IN 1595 A SPANIARD MAKING A MAP OF FLORIDA SKETCHED a canal from the Atlantic Ocean to the Gulf of Mexico. No such canal existed, but in the four hundred years since then many more people have envisioned a canal across the state.

Thomas Jefferson was the first president to express an interest in building a canal so that ships could avoid the long trip around the state. In the 1800s there were four studies about the possibility of building a canal and two more in 1913 and 1924, but they were all inconclusive.

A 1927 report contained enough enthusiasm for the project to encourage supporters. In 1935 five million dollars in federal relief money was authorized to start work on the canal, but not much was accomplished.

The following year Claude Pepper was elected to the Senate and became a champion of the canal. Year after year he pushed for the canal, which by then carried a price tag of nearly two hundred million dollars. Despite his efforts, there was too much opposition in the Senate. Pepper was defeated for reelection in 1950 and the canal lost its champion in Congress. But canal fans continued to push for their dream, and Congress finally gave approval.

In 1964 President Lyndon B. Johnson set off a dynamite blast near Palatka to start construction. Opponents, who had been focusing on cost and need, turned to ecological concerns. They charged that the canal would endanger the water supply south of the waterway. In 1970 the federal government put a fifteen-month moratorium on construction, and the following year President Nixon ordered all construction halted to preserve the environment.

139 | Saving the Cows Wreaked Havoc on the Environment

IN THE 1920S FLORIDA CATTLE BEGAN COMING DOWN WITH Texas tick fever. The result was one of the greatest assaults on Florida's environment and wildlife in the state's history. The state responded by requiring ranchers to dip their cattle in an arsenic solution every two weeks. It killed the ticks, but that was not all.

After the cows had been dipped the solution tended to drip downward along their flanks and end up on their stomachs. When it dried, their hides cracked. When it rained, the solution went into the soil and eventually worked its way into the water supply.

In Orange County the battle against the tick was especially brutal, taking nearly seven years. Because the dipping process was time consuming, many ranchers gave up. Often cows were simply shot and left in the fields. Ranchers thought they had eliminated tick fever, but a new strain appeared in 1935.

This time the ticks tended to attach themselves to white-tailed deer, not cows. The cows had resale value, so the ranchers wanted to save them. As for the deer, the state approved a campaign to eliminate them. Gunmen were hired to seek out the deer and kill them. Florida spent nearly three million dollars to kill the deer. It paid the gunmen eighty dollars per month, gave them supplies, and offered a bounty for each deer killed. They were allowed to use any method to hunt and kill the deer. With those sorts of incentives, the deer disappeared. They were killed off in most of central Florida, even though the infestation was limited.

The program was halted after national publications wrote about the carnage. The deer herds made a temporary comeback in south Florida. Their numbers increased until a new threat appeared in the 1960s, when the influx of human residents once again reduced the deer population.

140 A Plan to Promote Florida Turned Into an Embarrassment

IN 1891 PROMOTERS ORGANIZED A MASSIVE COLUMBIAN Exposition in Chicago. It would be the largest world's fair ever held. Each state was to be represented at the conference, and delegates were named.

On October 7, 1891, delegates from around Florida assembled in Orlando to consider how best to represent the state at the exposition. Florida's delegates decided to build a replica of the large Spanish fort at St. Augustine.

The organizers had to come up with about one hundred thousand dollars to pay for it. The legislature declined to appropriate any money for an exhibit. Various schemes were tried to raise the money, but they all failed.

The original organizers backed out, and the entire project fell to Arthur Jackson, a promoter and Florida booster. He could not raise the money, so organizers borrowed funds, primarily from Henry Flagler, the millionaire oil man.

The plans were changed; the fort would be smaller than originally planned. Construction began in September 1892 on the fort and exhibition building. The Florida buildings drew about twenty thousand visitors but had plenty of critics. The project featured displays of Florida products, including a huge chunk of phosphate and some plants.

One man said, "I have been to the Fair and am ashamed of Florida." Another said, "I think it would have been better not to have attempted anything than to have done what has been done." In Florida, soon everyone was blaming everyone for Florida's poor showing at the fair. The fair closed in October 1893. No one is sure what happened to the Florida building, but a couple of fires destroyed a number of structures and others were torn down.

141 A Tourist from Tampa Brought Yellow Fever to Jacksonville

A CENTURY AGO JACKSONVILLE WAS THE LARGEST CITY IN Florida and the business and tourism center. It drew about one hundred thousand tourists a year. In July 1888 an unwanted tourist arrived by train.

The visitor from Tampa checked into a hotel, but soon complained that he did not feel well. A doctor was called and found that the visitor had yellow fever. There was no known cure for the disease, and doctors did not even realize it was transmitted by mosquitos. Death could be slow and painful.

Threatening Jacksonville refugees

Within twenty-four hours the governor had quarantined the city. More cases were quickly reported. Soon there was hysteria. People began to escape the city secretly. Other cities did not want the Jacksonville refugees and armed patrols were formed to keep Jacksonville refugees away.

In Montgomery, Alabama, the mayor offered a reward for anyone turning in a Jacksonville refugee escaping the quarantine. Within a month eight people had died in Jacksonville. By September 1888 more than 150 of the twenty-five thousand residents had died and a coffin shortage developed. City leaders appealed for help.

The nation responded with contributions for food totaling more than three hundred thirty thousand dollars. Even President Grover Cleveland sent a check for two hundred dollars. As cold weather came the yellow fever epidemic abated. In December the quarantine was lifted. Nearly five-thousand cases had been reported and four-hundred thirty people had died.

And the man who started it all? He recovered and returned to Tampa.

142 The Pretty Little Plant That Turned Into a Nightmare

A MAN NAMED FULLER LIVED NEAR PALATKA ABOUT A CENtury ago. Fuller made a mistake that has come to haunt millions of people. He thought he was doing the people a favor and that his name would go down in the history books for his greatness.

Fuller brought the water hyacinth to Florida and turned it loose in the St. Johns River. At first it pleased everyone. Cattlemen thought it would be an excellent source of fodder and residents along the river thought its purple flowers were beautiful. The plants seemed to float along the river, and the passengers on passing steamboats could reach down and pick the flowers.

But there was more to the plant than its beautiful flowers. Below the water it was made of dense roots extending out as much as two feet. The plants also spread rapidly.

By 1883 a portion of the St. Johns near Palatka was covered by the plants. Boats could not pass, and by 1894 it was clear that the plant had become a menace to navigation and there were calls to Congress to do something about it.

In 1895 the government began efforts to control the hyacinth, attempts that continue to this day. A study found that the problem was even worse than originally thought. The government tried chemicals to kill the plants, but while the top of the plant quickly died, the part under the water remained alive. Next came another chemical that had no effect. Then an unsuccessful

A boat tries to pass through hyacinths

attempt was made to burn the plants. The government engineers tried crushing the plants. Crushing killed the plants but this proved to be too difficult.

Then it was back to chemicals, this time with a solution that actually worked on the plants. A former houseboat was used to spray the solution, but cattlemen complained that it killed their cows and convinced Congress to halt the spraying. Meanwhile the plant was spreading throughout the state. The plant made its way south, reaching Sanford. One steamboat spent three hours traveling just one hundred feet through the plants. By 1918 they had spread through the Kissimmee River and into Lake Okeechobee.

Since then dozens of ideas to eliminate the plant have been tried, including introducing bugs and fish to devour it. The hyacinth is still haunting Florida waterways. Fuller's gift to Florida turned into an expensive nightmare.

143 Some Were Held in Bondage Even after Slavery Ended

IN THE LATE 1800S THE FLORIDA LEGISLATURE PASSED A LAW that required workers who owed their employers money to keep working or be charged with a crime. The result was a system of legal peonage in which workers found themselves going deeper and deeper into debt each year and locked into brutal jobs. The worst offenders were the turpentine camp owners.

Life as a turpentine worker was miserable, and many workers were lured to work in turpentine camps without understanding what it involved. As soon as they arrived they found themselves in debt to their employers. Many of those lured to Florida turpentine camps were immigrants who had arrived in New York and were then brought to Florida. Gradually word reached New York about the conditions in Florida.

One of those who heard was Mary Grace Quackenbos, a New York reformer. In 1906 Quackenbos went to Florida to investigate the reports of men held in virtual slavery, beaten, and caged. Because she was well known, she used the name Grace Winterson and posed as a magazine reporter. What she found was worse than she had expected.

She immediately contacted the United States Department of Justice. At the same time, the United States attorney in Orlando, John Cheney, was also becoming interested in the issue. Quackenbos and Cheney had difficulty working together—she wanted to do a quick magazine story, he needed time to gather evidence.

Still, five workers of the Jackson Lumber Company in Pensacola were indicted for holding workers in peonage and sentenced to prison. Even President Theodore Roosevelt was drawn into the case, arguing against the "existence of virtual slavery in Southern Florida." Eventually Quackenbos was named a special assistant United States attorney to help prosecute the cases.

In Florida the criticism was directed at the critics of peonage. Newspapers and businesses banded together to create the impression that Florida was being picked on and slandered. Convictions became difficult to obtain. In Jacksonville the jury deliberated just seventeen minutes before finding eleven people accused of holding workers in peonage not guilty.

There were other legal setbacks, and eventually people lost interest in the peonage issue. Quackenbos returned to New York, where she continued to help workers. Florida laws governing contract labor remained on the books until 1944.

144   A Military Career Sank along with an Army Payroll

MAJOR JEREMIAH DASHIELL'S MILITARY CAREER WAS PROCEEDing nicely until he arrived in Florida. After two visits it was a shambles. Dashiell joined the army during the Mexican-American War. In 1855 he was in charge of a federal payroll being delivered by ship to troops near Ft. Myers.

Off Ft. Myers Dashiell transferred to a small boat for the trip to shore. The boat encountered swift currents and was quickly swamped. The six passengers—including Dashiell's young son—were rescued. The twenty-three-thousand-dollar payroll was lost. Dashiell explained his plight to the War Department and was absolved of responsibility.

Dashiell returned to South Carolina to pick up another payroll for the Florida troops, this time twenty-eight thousand dollars. He traveled by boat to the thriving port town of Palatka, where he left the money in his hotel room for just a few minutes. While he was gone somebody came in and took about half of it.

Dashiell returned to his room, not realizing he'd been robbed. He boarded his boat and moved on to New Smyrna. There he discovered that thirteen thousand dollars was missing. This time the government wanted its money. Dashiell went to Texas to sell some of his property to make up the loss, and while there, he received word that a slave might have stolen his money. He returned to Palatka but found that only three thousand dollars had been recovered. It also appeared that while the slave admitted taking forty-five hundred dollars, local businessmen might have walked off with the rest. The authorities were reluctant to prosecute, and no one was ever charged.

The War Department recommended that Dashiell be kicked out of the military, and in 1858 he was relieved of his duties. In 1963 some boys diving near Ft. Myers saw some bright objects on a reef. A closer look showed that they had found the gold coins lost a century before by Dashiell.

145 Mob Rule Was the Rule in Fighting Tampa Crime

IN 1860 A TAMPA NEWSPAPER COMPLAINED THAT THE CITY "was infested with gamblers, burglars, thieves, robbers and cutthroats." A group of residents responded with vigilante justice. The newspaper claimed that because of the vigilantes "robberies ceased, gamblers fled, riotness disappeared, and we can now say with pride and satisfaction, that there is not a town or county in the whole South, that can boast a more law-abiding people than the city of Tampa."

Mob justice was routine in Tampa, and lynchings were frequent. People complained to newspapers that too many people escaped prison or execution through legal technicalities or "dishonest lawyers." An Englishman passing through Tampa was charged with attempting to assault a young woman from a leading family. He was removed from jail and hanged. A local newspaper supported the lynching, saying it kept the victim from having to testify in court.

The lynch mob's leader was John Wall, a lawyer, former mayor, and newspaper editor. A federal judge, outraged at Wall's involvement in the lynching, issued an order preventing him from representing clients in federal court. His fellow lawyers were not as upset—they elected Wall the first president of the Florida Bar Association.

Eventually mob justice was used not only to punish criminals, but also to help leading businessmen. When workers went on strike at a cigar factory, the Tampa Board of Trade organized a committee to run strike leaders out of town. In 1901 another round of strikes prompted Tampa's leading citizens—including Wall—to kidnap fifteen strike leaders and load them on a boat that deposited them in Honduras.

After the turn of the century three Democratic politicians who tried to run for city council were abducted with the assistance of the police. They were tarred, feathered, and beaten, and one died. That was too much, even for Tampa. There was outrage in the community, and mob justice subsided.

---

146 Taking a Break for Lunch Became a Deadly Mistake

MAY 3, 1901, SEEMED LIKE SUCH A NICE DAY THAT THE watchman for the Cleveland Company in Jacksonville decided to join other workers for lunch.

There had been no rain in Jacksonville for more than a month, and everything was very dry. The Cleveland Company made fibers and used dried Spanish moss in the process. The moss was left out to dry in the Florida sun. The watchman was supposed to make sure that no sparks from nearby chimneys set the moss on fire.

While the workers ate, the moss caught fire. A worker tried to put out the fire, but it spread to a nearby warehouse. The fire department responded but a stiff wind overwhelmed their efforts. The fire was so huge that people in Savannah, Georgia, saw the black smoke and thought it was an approaching storm.

Families began to evacuate their homes. The streets were soon jammed with people fleeing the advancing flames. People jumped into the St. Johns River to avoid the fire. Fire departments from half a dozen cities were called on to help and spent eight hours bringing it under control. Seven people died in the fire, and thousands of people spent several nights sleeping on the ground.

The fire burned 148 square blocks in the city's center. At least ten thousand people lost their homes, and dozens of businesses were wiped out. Only about a third of the property destroyed was covered by insurance. In all nearly twenty-five hundred buildings were destroyed, including some of the city's most beautiful structures.

A relief organization was formed, and contributions poured in from throughout the country. Rebuilding efforts were quickly under way, and new construction began within hours of the fire.

147 Sarasota Is Still Waiting For Its Ship to Come In

THE TIMING COULD NOT HAVE BEEN WORSE. IT WAS JANUARY, 1926, when the city of Sarasota decided to throw away a million dollars. At the time the city thought it was investing the million in its bright future and that there would be a huge payoff. The city is still waiting for the payoff.

As early as 1912 Sarasota had begun dreaming of becoming a port city like Tampa or New Orleans. It did not seem to matter that there were already plenty of port cities along the Gulf of Mexico. The United States government laughed off Sarasota's plea for money to build a port, and the idea seemed to be dead.

Then, as land sales boomed throughout Florida in the 1920s, the dream of building the port was revived. A few souls asked what Sarasota would export and import, but they were shouted down by port supporters. The city had no idea where to get the money necessary to dredge a deep-water port. Then the newly formed Florida Power and Light Company of Miami came along. The company offered to purchase the city's electric company for about one million dollars. The city got the money and used it to start work on its deep-water port.

That was just as the Florida land boom burst. Prices fell as much as ninety percent, and some land could not be sold at any price. Sarasota hoped its new port would provide an economic cushion, but it was a disaster.

Only a few large ships ever used the port, and soon the shifting sands began to reclaim the dredged area. Things got so bad that the city of Sarasota even elected to get smaller, going from sixty-nine to seventeen square miles, because it could not afford to maintain the services needed in the larger area. So instead of reaping profits from their own city utility, they ended up with a worthless port paid for with the money from selling the utility.

BOOM AND BUST

Florida's 1920s Boom Sent Land Prices Soaring

SOME PEOPLE MADE FORTUNES, BUT MOST CAME OUT LOSERS in the biggest buying frenzy the state has ever seen. Anyone could buy a piece of property in Miami and Miami Beach with a small down payment, or "binder," and a promise to make a larger payment within thirty days. The idea was to sell the property for a large profit before the second payment was due. Usually the buyer could hardly afford the first payment, much less the second.

Most business deals were carried out on sidewalks. For a while the system seemed to work. Lots on Miami Beach that sold for seven thousand dollars in June were going for thirty-five thousand in July. Lots in downtown Miami that sold for a thousand dollars in the early 1900s were going for up to a million in 1925.

Promoters and their Miami development

One man said that while walking to work he purchased an apartment house for twenty thousand dollars by making a two-thousand-dollar down payment. He walked a few more blocks and found a buyer willing to pay thirty thousand dollars, a ten-thousand-dollar profit in a matter of minutes.

When a subdivision named Arch Creek started selling lots, there was a riot by buyers, who literally threw their money at salesmen. It really did not matter where the land was; buyers quickly bid for lots located in swamps miles west of Miami.

The end of the boom came quickly. In the fall of 1925 the Internal Revenue Service announced tax code changes that hurt the land speculators, and states began passing laws designed to protect residents who purchased Florida swampland sight unseen.

Even a mild slowdown in buying was disastrous. Those who had purchased on the binder system, and could not come up with a buyer, failed to make the second payment and defaulted. Almost as quickly as land prices had risen, they began to fall.

In September 1926 a hurricane with 125-mile-per-hour winds hit Miami, killing one hundred people and destroying thousands of homes. The boom was over, and the Great Depression settled in over Florida three years early.

149 Cedar Key Appeared to Be on Its Way to Greatness

TODAY PEOPLE USE WORDS LIKE "CHARMING" OR "RUSTIC" TO describe Cedar Key. Nobody uses the term "industrial center." For a while in the mid-1800s it looked as if the community on the Gulf of Mexico midway between St. Petersburg and Tallahassee might become a big city.

Cedar Key started in the 1840s as a summer resort. It also turned out to be an excellent spot for fishing and became a commercial fishing center. The timber in the area was perfect for making pencils, and Eberhard Faber purchased huge tracts of land to supply his New Jersey pencil factory and set up a sawmill to process the cedar.

Next came the turpentine and rosin industry. The pine and cypress trees soon drew the attention of the lumber industry. The goods were shipped from Cedar Key, and in 1860 a railroad opened connecting Fernandina to Cedar Key.

During the Civil War the town was blockaded by the U.S. Navy. In January 1862 a Union patrol attacked the town and destroyed the wharf, shops, and the turpentine factories. After the war the population increased steadily, peaking in 1885 at five thousand and making it one of the state's largest cities.

By 1889 Cedar Key was running out of natural resources. The heavy forests of trees were gone. No one had thought to replant during the boom years. The fishermen had cleaned out the oyster beds and fishing areas, and the population began to decline.

By 1900 Cedar Key had only 864 residents. The population is about the same today. There is a museum in Cedar Key, which capture the flavor of the old town.

150   Once Upon a Time, Juno Seemed to Be a City on the Rise

THE NAME JUST DOES NOT SOUND RIGHT: THE JUNO Dolphins, the University of Juno. But that's the way it was—almost.

Around 1890, when Dade County included what is now Palm Beach County, folks who lived in the northern part were unhappy that the county seat was in Miami, claiming they were not getting their share of services. So they held an election, and to everyone's surprise the voters decided to move the county seat out of Miami.

The question was where. Somebody offered some land for a courthouse, and they named the new county seat Juno. There was a town called Jupiter about eight miles away, and as every student of Roman mythology knows, Juno was the wife of Jupiter.

There was even a little railroad connecting the two towns. The railroad was so small that the train did not bother to turn around—it went forward to Juno and backed up to Jupiter. In keeping with the Roman mythology theme, the towns of Mars and Venus were created along the train line. Venus ended up with one resident, while Mars never had anybody living there.

A courthouse was built in Juno, a newspaper started, and some businesses opened. Unfortunately, a second railroad was built that bypassed Juno, and soon the small railroad was out of business. Without a railroad it was difficult to get to Juno, and most people stopped going unless they had business at the courthouse. The voters had only agreed to move the county seat there as an experiment for ten years, and everyone knew it would return to Miami.

The property became worthless, and people simply walked away. The hotel and saloon were abandoned. The jungle began to reclaim the area. In 1899 the county seat moved back to Miami and it was all over for Juno. It was never incorporated as a

The Jupiter to Juno train

town; never had more than two dozen residents and had no church, doctor, or bank.

What was left of Juno burned to the ground. There was a bronze plaque where the village stood, but somebody stole it and the stone marker that held it was knocked down by a truck. And thus Juno fell.

151 Belmore: A Promoter's Dream Vanished without a Trace

IN THE PAST CENTURY HUNDREDS OF TOWNS HAVE STARTED in Florida, only to die and disappear. One of those is Belmore, launched in 1885 about forty miles south of Jacksonville. It was largely a land promoter's dream.

Town organizers divided their property into lots, then launched a newspaper, the *Belmore Florida Journal,* to help promote the property. A copy of the third issue of the paper showed what the new town was like. The edition, printed in February 1886, carried several favorable stories about the prospects for land values in the area.

According to a letter in the *Journal,* there were about fifty residents in the town and the major industry was a sawmill. But the town was immersed in controversy. One letter from a Belmore resident states, "We have good soil and water—jealousy and false newspaper reports to the contrary—and as fine a climate as there is in the world. . . . Do not listen to all the false reports, especially about Belmore, which are constantly circulated and used to induce people to go farther South."

The owners of Belmore, a Chicago-based company, sold city lots for ten dollars apiece. Each lot was forty feet by one hundred feet. The company claimed buying a lot was "a safe speculation. No chance to lose, but sure opportunity to make big money on a small investment."

Land outside the city was offered for twenty dollars to fifty dollars an acre. The newspaper had a section about people in the community: "Mr. J. H. Ross, the agent of the Belmore Land Co., has gained thirty pounds since coming to Belmore, Nov. 1."

The newspaper claimed that Belmore was a good place to grow oranges and had excellent timber. A freeze a few years later wiped out the orange crop, and growers were forced farther south. The timber was cut, and the sawmill closed. As late as 1915 there was a four-room schoolhouse in Belmore, but gradually the town disappeared.

IF YOU HAD BEEN A REAL ESTATE PROMOTER A CENTURY AND a half ago, you probably would have passed up the chance to buy land in places like Tampa, Orlando, and Miami, and invested your fortune in St. Joseph. Or you might have bought a few lots in Apalachicola and waited for the profits to roll in.

You would still be waiting. Florida, with its history of boom and bust, has seen dozens of cities come and go. Yesterday's city of the future has become today's overgrown swamp.

The best-known unknown city was St. Joseph, west of Tallahassee in Gulf County. In the 1830s it appeared to be on its way to becoming the state capital. The state's first constitution was written there. The port became the richest on the Gulf Coast. There was a thriving downtown, and mansions were built by those who had made fortunes in shipping.

In 1841 a ship from South America docked in St. Joseph. At least one of the crew members had yellow fever. The disease quickly spread through the town. Within weeks nearly seventy-five percent of the residents, who may have numbered about two thousand, had come down with yellow fever. Those who did not want to risk contracting the disease fled. So great was the fear of yellow fever that no one who fled returned to the town for three years.

As a few folks began to return, a hurricane struck and washed most of the town out to sea. A few additional storms removed all traces of the town except for a cemetery. By 1854 anyone standing where St. Joseph had once been never would have known a city had been there.

Apalachicola, also on the Gulf Coast, was the third-largest cotton port along the coast in 1840. Its daily newspaper was one of the most influential in the South, and its downtown was the largest in Florida. The population numbered about two thousand. During the Civil War Union forces blockaded the town. When Confederate defenders were withdrawn to fight against General William Sherman's army, most of the citizens fled—and did not return. The town was taken by Union troops, and Apalachicola declined in importance.

TURNING SWAMPLAND INTO LUXURY HOME SITES MADE A fortune for D. P. Davis. It also left him broke. Davis got his start in Tampa, creating Davis Island in Tampa Bay during the land-boom years of the early 1920s.

He dumped millions of tons of dirt into a marshy area and ended up with hundreds of waterfront lots. His venture was so successful that he began looking for another low-lying area. In 1925 he came to Anastasia Island opposite St. Augustine.

The area had a wonderful view of the old Spanish fort and the historic downtown, but it was under water. That did not stop Davis. He announced grand plans for twenty-two hundred lots, a golf course, apartment houses, a grand hotel, a yacht club, and a casino. Davis began buying land—about fifteen hundred acres on the northern end of the island.

Dredging began in late 1925. An eighteen-thousand-ton dredge was brought in to fill the marshland, but a second dredge was needed to finish the job. About six acres of new land were created each day. Davis selected Friday, the thirteenth of November, to begin selling his lots.

It was an unlucky day. Just as the lots went on sale, the Florida land boom was coming to an end. Although Davis was a millionaire, he was a paper millionaire. He had sold thousands of lots in Tampa, but the buyers had usually turned over a small down payment and made monthly payments.

When the boom went bust, the buyers stopped making their payments. Lot sales were slow, and in August 1926 Davis lost control of his Tampa property.

In October Davis went to Europe. He said he wanted to look into developing off-shore property there. While sailing across the ocean he was lost at sea. Whether Davis killed himself or accidentally fell overboard has never been determined.

His project managers tried to carry on. A few families moved in, but the project lacked the money to continue. One homeowner found that while he

D. P. Davis, right

had purchased a lot that was supposed to be on a canal, there was no canal.

By 1927 the land boom had collapsed, and Davis Shores went with it. The company went bankrupt with more than a million dollars in debts. It was not until after World War II that development began again on Davis Shores. Today there are only a few vacant lots left there.

154 — Florida's First Promoter Ended Up Broke and Insane

PETER SMITH WAS WEALTHY. ALONG WITH HIS PARTNER, John Jacob Astor, Smith had made a fortune in land speculation in the late 1700s. One of those deals involved purchasing land from an Oneida Indian chief named Skenandoah. The deal was so good that Smith named his son Peter Skenandoah Smith.

Like his father, the younger Smith started out a success, but he ended up broke and insane. Around 1830 the younger Smith came to St. Augustine seeking a new start. He became the state's first promoter. He sent letters to Northern newspapers extolling the virtues of moving to Florida and promoting land sales.

Smith became active in the community, contributing to local causes, setting up a real estate firm, and building the community's first housing development. He became the largest developer in St. Augustine, built a mansion, and became a power in the community.

The publisher of the local newspaper found himself thrown out of the Presbyterian Church after criticizing Smith. Then came the Panic of 1837: People went broke and banks everywhere failed. In Florida, bankers were so hated that a constitutional amendment was passed denying elective office to any bank officer.

Peter Smith lost his fortune overnight. His creditors wanted him arrested. He put his mansion up for sale, and one by one his properties were auctioned off. Smith fled the state, one step ahead of his creditors and the sheriff.

He moved to Philadelphia and became involved in a series of slightly nutty causes. Eventually he went insane and died in 1858 of what was described as a brain disease. He left behind plenty of buildings in St. Augustine. His mansion was turned into a hotel and survived until after World War II. His housing development remains and is on the National Register of Historic Places. Unfortunately, the register mistakenly gives the credit to another developer. And in the unkindest cut of all, the street that was named for him—Skenandoah—was changed by a sign painter who obviously thought someone had made a spelling error. It is now called Shenandoah.

155 The Developers' Dreams for a City Were Lost in a Storm

IT WAS TO BE A DREAM CITY. THE DEVELOPERS BOUGHT land on the Gulf of Mexico, laid out home sites, and began to sell lots to eager buyers. A city soon sprang up. Then a violent storm wiped out the town. The town was Port Leon, which disappeared in 1843.

Organizers of Port Leon thought the location on the Panhandle coast near the town of St. Marks would be perfect. The latter had become such a major shipping center that its small harbor was frequently filled, and Port Leon would be able to handle the overflow.

There was already a railroad running to St. Marks, and in 1839 the railroad was extended to Port Leon. Businesses opened and docks and warehouses were built to serve the ships that anchored in the port. The town even had a weekly newspaper.

On September 13, 1843, a strong wind began shortly before noon. It created an unusually high tide, but nothing to alarm the residents of the town. In the afternoon the strong wind died down and the storm seemed to be over.

Around midnight the wind picked up again, eventually reaching hurricane force. A huge tidal surge of almost ten feet swamped the town. The eye of the storm passed, bringing with it the usual calm. Then the rest of the hurricane passed over Port Leon.

All but one of the city's warehouses were destroyed. Almost every house was leveled; stores and the goods inside were nearly a total loss. Only one person died, a young boy. The railroad was washed away, and St. Marks itself suffered extensive damage.

After the citizens of Port Leon had assessed the damage, they gathered to decide what to do. They voted to call it quits and move to another place. They selected a site to the north and called it Newport. It was located at a higher elevation and considered safer in case of a storm. The town of Port Leon vanished.

156 Key West Survived Grim Times before Its Comeback

THE 1920S WERE A GRIM TIME FOR KEY WEST. THE U.S. government dramatically reduced the military presence there, and the cigar makers and sponge divers also left. Key West was left without any industry, and the population declined. When the Great Depression came along things got worse. By 1933 Key West had a deficit of five million dollars and no way to make payments. In 1934 the city asked that a state of emergency be declared and that the federal government take over.

The Federal Emergency Relief Administration moved in and quickly sized up the situation: Key West needed tourists in order to survive. The government began rehabilitating the city. City residents donated more than one million hours of labor and learned how to manufacture items for tourists. Unemployed artists were hired to decorate the city.

Tourists began arriving in droves. Then the city's comeback was halted.

On September 2, 1935, a hurricane was making its way into the Gulf of Mexico. Forecasters thought it would pass well south of the keys. Instead, it passed over Key West at the worst possible time. Because of the Labor Day holiday there were no forecasters working to warn of the storm's arrival. Rescue officials were also off duty. By the time a train was sent to remove residents, the storm was at its height. The train was knocked off the tracks and much of the track demolished.

About six hundred World War I veterans were working in the Keys as part of the rehabilitation program. They had no warning of the storm, and as a result 238 died, as did one hundred Key Westers. The railroad was never rebuilt. Its road bed was used for a highway from Miami to Key West that is still in use.

Later, tourists began to return. World War II brought back the military, and the population increased. The property nobody wanted in the 1930s has become some of the most valuable in the state.

157 The Depression Ended Howey's Dream of a City and Political Offices

WILLIAM HOWEY HAD TRIED JUST ABOUT EVERYTHING BEFORE he arrived in Florida in 1908. He had even tried growing pineapples in Mexico in 1907, but a revolution forced him to leave. When he got to Florida, Howey sold land near Winter Haven, where he learned about the citrus industry. He moved his operation to Lake County and by 1920 acquired nearly sixty thousand acres.

His development was unusual. Howey purchased land for about ten dollars an acre, planted forty-eight citrus trees on each acre, then sold the land for nearly a thousand dollars an acre. An investor would buy the land and the orange trees. Profits from the orange crops would go to the investor. If, after ten years, the oranges did not provide the revenue Howey had promised, he would buy the land back.

To lure buyers, Howey led a motor caravan from Chicago to Lake

County. He named his development Howey-in-the-Hills. Unlike a lot of developers, Howey was able to survive the land bust of 1926: He had a hotel that attracted lots of tourists, and orange sales continued to rise.

In 1928 Howey ran for governor as a Republican, promising to cut taxes and spending. Thanks to the nationwide strength of Republican presidential candidate Herbert Hoover, Howey gathered an impressive thirty-nine percent of the vote. Four years later Howey ran again, but this time he received just thirty-three percent of the vote. His popularity had declined along with that of the GOP following the stock market crash in 1929.

Howey's land sales nearly stopped as the Depression worsened. He was forced to lay off most of his employees, and his community defaulted on its bonds.

Howey died in 1938. After his death the Securities and Exchange Commission ruled that Howey's method of selling orange groves and land amounted to selling unregistered securities and was illegal. It wasn't until after his death that his community achieved the goals of growth and prosperity that he had set for it half a century earlier.

158 One-Time Clown John Ringling's Last Years Weren't Much Fun

WHEN JOHN RINGLING ARRIVED IN SARASOTA IN 1911 HE was riding high. His family's circus had survived tough competition in the 1880s. By 1907 the family was able to buy out the Barnum & Bailey Circus and create the most profitable circus in the country.

Ringling, who began his career as a clown in the family circus, spent a lot of time traveling and looking for business investments. In Sarasota he found good, cheap land—more than sixty thousand acres—and soon his brothers started buying it. Land on Florida's west coast was much less expensive than land on the east coast.

To promote the west coast, Ringling hit upon an idea: He invited his good friend President Warren G. Harding down for a visit. Ringling thought one of the keys off Sarasota would make a perfect site for a winter White House, and the presence of the president several months a year would almost guarantee successful land sales. Harding thought a visit would be a splendid idea. Unfortunately for Ringling, Harding died shortly before the anticipated visit.

Ringling's brother Charles built an eight-hundred-thousand-dollar marble palace. John followed with his own mansion, which cost one million dollars. In 1926 the land boom went bust, but the Ringlings survived without much trouble, even though land prices in Sarasota fell dramatically.

To prop up the economy Ringling moved the circus' winter head-quarters from Connecticut to Sarasota. Then things began to go wrong for John Ringling. His wife died, and a second marriage ended in a quick divorce and two hundred thousand dollars in legal bills. His financial situation deteriorated during the Depression. The bank he owned failed, and he lost control of his circus. Even his telephone was cut off for non-payment of bills.

A court ordered his estate to be sold on December 7, 1936. Five days before the auction was to be held Ringling died. Although he had only three hundred dollars in cash when he died, he was still worth millions, more than enough to pay all of his creditors.

The work of untangling Ringling's financial affairs took nearly a decade. The state of Florida ended up with the Ringling estate, part of which has been turned into a college of art—just what John Ringling had in mind.

159 For a Quarter an Acre, Hamilton Disston Bailed Out Florida

IF THERE WERE A HALL OF FAME FOR SWEET LAND DEALS, Florida's entry doubtless would be the purchase of property that was to become the Disston sugar plantation near Kissimmee.

In 1881 Florida was one million dollars in debt. With a massive debt payment coming due, Governor William Bloxham conceived a land sale as the solution to the state's fiscal problems. Florida owned twenty million acres of land and Bloxham figured he could unload a portion of that and save the state from bankruptcy.

That was where Hamilton Disston, a Philadelphia millionaire who loved to fish in the lakes around Kissimmee, came in. The state offered to sell Disston four million acres, including the lakes, for twenty-five cents an acre.

He accepted the offer and agreed to drain the swampy areas. By 1885 Disston's agents were advertising land, much of it reclaimed, near the Kissimmee River for $1.25 an acre. One of Disston's early projects involved what is today East Lake Tohopekaliga. He turned that from a cypress swamp into a smaller body of water with a beach.

Disston also started a massive sugar growing and milling operation near St. Cloud. He built a railroad and encouraged tourism but encountered problems. Changing federal laws regarding sugar imports played havoc with domestic sugar prices, and Disston's sugar profits began to sour.

In the panic of 1893 Disston lost part of his fortune. When he died in 1896, his family let the sugar empire dissolve. The mill fell into disuse, the machinery was sold, and the company stopped paying its bills. Disston's name soon faded, and little remains today to mark his once huge empire.

BUILDING
FLORIDA'S CITIES

**Population Shift Changes Lineup
for Largest Cities**

THE 1990 CENSUS FIGURES SHOW THAT FLORIDA'S POPULA-
tion once again grew dramatically. The lineup of major cities remained
about the same. Jacksonville is the largest, Miami is second, Tampa is
third, and St. Petersburg is fourth. That has been the lineup since 1970
when Jacksonville increased the size of its city to include most of Duval
County, passing Miami.

For the past half century, Orlando and Ft. Lauderdale have battled for
the fifth spot. The figures show how cities rise and fall. Consider Key
West. Up until 1900, Key West was Florida's largest city. In 1890, it had
18,000 hearty residents. Its population reached its peak in 1960 with
34,000 residents. Now, it's down to about 24,000 residents.

Florida's second largest city for most of the 1800s was St Augustine
with a couple of thousand people. As late as 1910, St. Augustine was one
of Florida's five largest cities. Key West remained in the top five until
1930. Jacksonville, which didn't make the top-five list until 1880, became
the largest city in 1900. St. Petersburg first made the list in 1920, and has
been he fourth largest city in every census since 1930.

Tampa joined the top five in 1870. Tallahassee was in the top five until
1900. City populations can be misleading. In Jacksonville the population
includes large numbers of suburban residents. In Orlando, it does not.

In 1890, Orlando had a population of 3,000, the same as Tallahassee
and good enough for sixth place. As late as 1910, Orlando and Sanford
were tied in population. In 1920 it was still close, and it was not until the
1930s that Orlando began to pull away.

The 1920s were a boom time for many Florida cities. People bought
Florida land for investments and vacation homes. That meant that the
population exploded in cities designed to lure tourists, such as Miami,
Daytona Beach, and Clearwater. Clearwater's population increased 400

percent between 1920 and 1930. Miami had a population of 5,000 in 1910 and 110,000 in 1930. Daytona Beach had 1,000 residents in 1920 and 17,000 by 1930.

At the same time, most of the older North Florida cities saw their population remain the same or grow slowly. Gainesville, the fourth largest city in 1910, added just a thousand residents over the next ten years, while Miami added 25,000.

161   Olds Turned from Cars to Florida Real Estate

BACK IN 1898, A FELLOW FROM MICHIGAN WAS CONCERNED about his parents. They were getting old and he thought a warmer climate might help them live longer. So he bought a house at 129 North Halifax near Daytona Beach. Money was not a problem since the man, Ransom E. Olds, had begun manufacturing automobiles in 1887, well before Henry Ford set up shop.

While about one out of twenty-five Americans drive an Oldsmobile today, Olds is little remembered as an automotive pioneer. He had some trouble with his car company, his need for cash forced him to sell large portions of his firm, and eventually he and his partners had a falling out. Olds left in 1904, before the really big money began to roll in. In 1908 the company was sold to General Motors.

In the early 1920s, Olds decided to create a retirement city, not for the wealthy, but for the middle class. It would be a planned community with neat homes, parks, and health-care facilities. He purchased twenty thousand acres on Tampa Bay and named it Oldsmar. Then he began building. Unfortunately, the Florida land boom turned into the land bust of 1926, and nobody showed much interest in his Florida land.

In one of the worst land deals of the century, Olds traded his land for a building in St. Louis. Today Oldsmar has a large racetrack and a population

The Oldsmar sales force in 1925

of 8,600. Olds maintained his interest in Florida, however, buying orange groves. In 1943 he started a retirement home for ministers in Daytona Beach. Olds died in 1950 at the age of 86.

His Idea for a City Failed, But His Road Succeeded

AROUND THE TURN OF THE CENTURY, FLORIDA WAS THE WINter home of some of the nation's wealthiest people, leaders of American industry such as John D. Rockefeller. In 1902, these barons of capitalism were joined by W. J. Conners, who looked decidedly out of place.

Conners, whose nickname was "Fingy," had joined the crew of a Great Lakes steamer ship at the age of thirteen and sailed to Buffalo, New York, where he took a job as a stevedore. He was tough and worked his way up to become leader of the stevedore union and became very wealthy. He became the model for the character "Jiggs," the portly father in the comic strip, "Bringing Up Father." Along with other wealthy people, Conners started going to Florida to get some sun. And, like his fellow millionaires from industry, Conners began buying Florida land. In 1917 he purchased 4,000 acres near West Palm Beach. His idea was to farm the land, but the farm failed.

He bought more land and named the area for himself, Connersville. It also failed to produce any money from farming or land sales. Unwilling to give up, he purchased the entire town of Okeechobee from the Florida East Coast Railway in 1924. There were only two ways to reach Okeechobee, by train or horse. Conners decided that if people were to flock to his new town there would have to be a road from the east.

He spent about $1 million in an unsuccessful attempt at road building, then hired some professionals to do the job. In 1924 the road was opened and became a success. He charged a $1.50 toll—a high price in those days—but the demand was incredible. On the first day, 3,000 cars used it, and it routinely took in about $2,000 a day. The road attracted people who had never been able to drive across the swamps to Okeechobee.

While the road was a success, his dream of creating a new Chicago on the banks of Lake Okeechobee failed. Conners died in 1929, and in 1930 the state purchased his road—now State Road 710.

Naming Cities Involved Borrowing Old Names

WHEN PEOPLE CAME TO AMERICA FROM OTHER NATIONS, they often adopted names from their old countries for cities here. Plymouth is a city in England and in Massachusetts. New Hampshire is a state, while the original Hampshire is in England.

When people moved from the North to Florida, they often brought the names of their communities with them. Consider the Lake County town of Altoona, which was named by Thomas Hinson, who was from Altoona, Pennsylvania. The small community of Englewood near Sarasota was named by the three brothers from Englewood, Illinois, who created the town. Citizens from Auburndale, Massachusetts, changed the name of the Polk County town of Sanatoria to Auburndale.

A group of farmers from Bowling Green, Kentucky, purchased large holdings in the Hardee County community of Utica in the late 1880s and changed the name to Bowling Green. The community of Keystone Heights has had two names from the North. It was originally called Brooklyn, but in 1922 a Pittsburgh native arrived and wanted the name changed to the nickname of his home state.

La Crosse, near Gainesville, was settled by people from La Crosse, Wisconsin, and Newberry, also near Gainesville, was named for Newberry, South Carolina. Longwood, in Seminole County, was the name of a neighborhood in Boston. When a group from Detroit moved to Florida in 1913, they wanted to name their Dade County community for their hometown. The post office said it would be too confusing and the group selected Florida City.

The small community of Golf in Palm Beach County was named by residents for a town in Illinois. Umatilla in Lake County is named for Umatilla, Oregon. Valparaiso in Okaloosa County is named for Valparaiso, Indiana.

Some names came from Europe. Dundee in Pinellas County is named for a town in Scotland. A. F. Wrotniski, who had been born in Clermont, France, named Clermont in Lake County. A group from Holland settled in Broward County and selected the name Hollandale, but it was some-how changed to Hallandale.

164 Sanford's Fortune Built the Orange Industry

HENRY SHELTON SANFORD WAS BORN INTO A CONNECTICUT family that made its fortune manufacturing brass tacks. The Civil War increased Sanford's wealth as the demand for brass soared. When the war ended, Sanford's income from war-related products—such as brass used for shells—fell sharply. He flirted with owning a sugar plantation in Louisiana, but it burned down. When he tried to grow cotton in South Carolina, the crop was wiped out by caterpillars

Sanford turned to Florida. In 1870 he purchased 12,500 acres on Lake Monroe and named a small settlement there after himself. He began laying out city lots and grove sites; buildings began to rise along the lake. Sanford planted cotton, but the caterpillars that wiped out his South Carolina crop moved south and destroyed his Florida crop. Sanford's only success came from his orange groves. In many ways, Sanford was the creator of the modern orange industry. His groves were superior to anything ever seen in the state and other growers began to follow his techniques.

Sanford's Florida projects as a whole were a drain on his resources. To help pay the bills, he took on partners which only produced disagreements. Finally, Sanford gave up. When he died in 1891, his fortune was almost gone and he was facing bankruptcy.

One year later, his Florida company gave up, selling off what remained of its holdings. A decade later, Sanford's once magnificent groves were sold for just $1,000.

Except for Sanford himself, no member of his family ever lived in the town that bears his name.

165 Flagler Saw the Attraction Florida Held for Tourists

IN THE WINTER OF 1884, HENRY M. FLAGLER ARRIVED IN ST. Augustine. He was one of the wealthiest men in the world, a partner in the Standard Oil Company with John D. Rockefeller. Flagler came to spend his honeymoon with his second wife. He remained a short time, but the memories of the city stuck with him. A year later, he returned and decided to build a hotel as a winter resort for his wealthy friends.

He wanted St. Augustine to become the American Riviera, and started by building a huge hotel. When the hotel opened in January 1888, it marked the opening of Florida as a major tourist mecca. The Ponce de Leon Hotel was just the start of Flagler's plan for St. Augustine.

Flagler's Ponce de Leon Hotel

Across the street he built another hotel, the Alcazar. It was smaller and less ornate, but featured shops, a huge indoor swimming pool, and a gymnasium. Flagler also took over a nearby hotel when its owner went bankrupt. He renamed it the Cordova.

Transportation to St.

Augustine was primitive and Flagler's wealthy guests wanted to travel in style. He purchased a railroad from St. Augustine to the St. Johns River and connected it to the rail center in Jacksonville. After a thirty-five-hour rail journey, passengers from New York City arrived in St. Augustine in style. From the train station, the guests traveled by carriage on streets paved by Flagler.

He also built a baseball field, laundry, dairy, and Episcopal and Methodist churches. He even owned the hospital and city hall. The city's population doubled almost overnight, and the city took on debt to expand its fire department and other city services.

The hotel drew the wealthy for grand balls. Even President Grover Cleveland showed up. There was one thing Flagler's money could not guarantee, the weather. Flagler began looking South for a warmer spot. Flagler extended his railroad to Ormond Beach, then to Palm Beach and Miami and finally to Key West. Along the way he built more grand hotels. In 1893, a nationwide depression reduced tourism in St. Augustine, even among the rich. By 1894, Flagler had turned his attentions from St. Augustine entirely. Its days as the American Riviera were over, just six years after they began.

166 She Convinced Flagler to Turn Miami into a City

WHEN JULIA TUTTLE FIRST SAW MIAMI IN THE EARLY 1870S, there was not much to see. The city had only a couple hundred residents. Still, something suggested to the Cleveland native that Miami might someday be more than a village. She returned to Miami from time to time to visit, and several years later, after the death of her husband, she decided to live there.

Julia Tuttle

Tuttle purchased 640 acres on the north bank of the Miami River, land that today is the heart of downtown Miami. She hoped people would move to the area and build houses on the land, even though in the 1890s few people wanted to live in Miami. The heat and mosquitoes were unbearable, and Miami was difficult to reach. What Tuttle needed was a railroad to bring in the visitors. She knew that Henry Flagler's railroad had turned villages like Palm Beach into popular resorts, and she wanted Flagler to extend his railroad to Miami.

He thought the idea was preposterous. Then, in 1895, her opportunity came. A severe freeze destroyed crops as far south as Palm Beach. Tuttle went outside her home, picked some flowers, wrapped them in damp cotton and sent them to Flagler in St. Augustine.

He was amazed that the freeze that had caused so much damage in Palm Beach had left Miami untouched. He decided to extend his railroad and build the Royal Palm Hotel on land donated by Tuttle. She thought it was the beginning of a great city and urged Flagler to support her idea of laying out wide streets. Flagler said: "It would be silly. This place will never be anything more than a fishing village for my hotel guests!"

In April 1896, the first trains reached Miami. The next month, the first newspaper appeared. In July, the 343 voters decided to incorporate. Tuttle turned out to be right, but she did not live long enough to see her city prosper. She died in 1898 at age fifty.

167 Miami Beach Went from Mangrove Swamp to Resort

CARL FISHER HAD A KNACK FOR MAKING A BUSINESS BOOM. He sold newspapers on a train by flashing photos of naked women. He publicized his bike store by pedaling across a wire twelve stories high, and he drove a car off the tallest building in Indianapolis to push his car-repair business.

He perfected the automobile headlight and in 1911 sold his invention to Union Carbide for $5 million. With that money, he built the Indianapolis Speedway and bought a mangrove swamp in South Florida. The swamp was called Miami Beach.

He hauled in sand and made the swamp a real beach, added a golf course, speedboat races, and tennis courts, but lot sales were very slow. He imported beautiful young women, dressed them in the skimpiest bathing suits the law would allow and sent their pictures all over the country. Still, sales lagged. Years passed without much success, but Fisher would not give up.

He cast about for a stunt to bring his resort nationwide publicity. In 1921, the president-elect, Warren G. Harding, was vacationing in St. Augustine. Fisher sent his secretary, a beautiful young woman, to deliver the invitation. Harding was impressed and agreed to visit Miami Beach. The resulting publicity was tremendous. News photographers shot Harding swimming, lying in the sun, playing golf, using an elephant for a caddy. Business boomed and Fisher had won again.

168 A Fortune in Champagne Created the Town of DeBary

FOR MILLIONS OF AMERICANS, A SPECIAL OCCASION CALLS FOR a glass of champagne. That is why there's a town in Volusia County named DeBary. Baron Frederick DeBary was born in Germany in 1815. At the age of twenty-five, he was hired by the Mumm family to sell its champagnes and wines in the United States.

Young Debary was a success, selling Mumm brands to the rising class of wealthy Americans. He became a millionaire and in 1870 came to Florida to vacation on the St. Johns River.

He purchased land on Lake Monroe and built a mansion, which included one of the first elevators installed in a home. He entertained the famous, including presidents Ulysses S. Grant and Grover Cleveland. He developed a steamship company that helped open up Florida's interior to commerce.

That venture led him into the orange business, and he made even more money from what were designed to be merely hobbies. DeBary died in 1898, and his estate remained in his family until World War II. A battle among the heirs forced the sale of the home and land to a development company that built the community of DeBary. In 1959 DeBary's original house was deeded to the Florida Federation of Art, and in 1967 it became a historic memorial and was restored by the state.

169 Curtiss Went from Planes to Cows in Opa-Locka

GLENN CURTISS MADE A SENSATIONAL FIRST IMPRESSION ON Florida. In 1907 he raced his motorcycle at 137 miles per hour on Ormond Beach. No human had ever gone faster. He moved on to Miami and made a more lasting impression experimenting with seaplanes and developing real estate.

Because the water system in South Florida left a lot to be desired, Curtiss drank canned milk. Not one to do things on a small scale, he did more than merely drink it. He purchased 120,000 acres at two and three dollars an acre and started raising cows. His dairy business was a success, but the land became too valuable for cows.

He sold his airplane company for $32 million and went into the land business. His timing was perfect. The Florida land boom of the 1920s was under way and in ten days he sold $1 million in lots. Curtiss formed the city of Hialeah, then formed a second city, which is now called Miami Springs.

It was Curtiss who thought of building his homes around a golf course with winding roads. His third city was supposed to be his most magnificent. The tract of land was called Opatishawockalocka, which everyone called Opa-Locka. Curtiss designed the city buildings to resemble those found in the Arabian Nights fables. He named the streets Sinbad, Ali Baba, and Sultan and built a city hall with six domes. Only a few lots had been sold when the bottom dropped out of the Florida land market in 1926.

His dream city fell into disrepair and Curtiss pulled out. Curtiss gave some of his land to the city of Miami to build what is now Miami International Airport.

170 A Place of Beauty Was a Scene of Tragedy

THE BEACH AT NEW SMYRNA IS BEAUTIFUL. IT IS SO LOVELY that it is difficult to imagine the horror that took place there more than two hundred years ago. In 1768, Florida was in the hands of the British, who were trying to lure colonists. Along came Dr. Andrew Turnbull from London with a scheme. If the British would give him 100,000 acres around what is now Daytona Beach, he would import colonists from the Mediterranean to produce cotton, silk, and indigo.

Although the colony could support only five hundred people, Turnbull recruited 1,400 men, women, and children from Greece, Italy, and Spain. Nearly 150 died of hunger on the voyage over. When the colonists arrived, they were put to work clearing the land and they were forced to exist almost entirely on grits. The overseers were cruel and floggings were frequent. The conditions became so oppressive that several hundred colonists revolted, overpowered the overseers, and tried to escape by ship.

They were captured and three of the leaders sentenced to death. One leader was told he could live if he agreed to execute the other two. He agreed only after the two other condemned men urged him to save himself. Within two years, more than half of the colonists who had set sail for Florida had died.

Turnbull lived lavishly—too lavishly as it turned out. His partners in England wanted to know why profits were not higher. An investigation uncovered the inhuman conditions in the colony. Turnbull was ordered arrested, but he escaped to South Carolina. The colony disbanded, and ten years after they left their native countries, just 291 of the original 1,400 colonists were still alive.

He Used His Newspaper to Build St. Petersburg

WILLIAM STRAUB SEEMED OUT OF PLACE WHEN HE ARRIVED in St. Petersburg in 1900. He could look at the scruffy little town of 7,300 people and see a major city. In 1901 he purchased the weekly *St. Petersburg Times* and turned it into a daily newspaper.

Then he began his campaigns. He turned his attention to the St. Petersburg waterfront. He wanted to protect the waterfront from eventual overdevelopment although that was not much of a threat in the early 1900s. His idea was to have the city own the port. He used his paper's editorial page to push for public ownership of the port, throwing himself into conflict with some of the region's most powerful people. In 1908, the city council agreed to acquire the port.

Straub convinced the city to hire a professional planner to develop a blueprint for the city's growth. The planner was hired, and he laid out streets and parks for a major city. He also campaigned to have the St. Petersburg area removed from Hillsborough County. Tampa was the major city in the county, and St. Petersburg was usually overlooked when it came to services. The residents of the St. Petersburg area paid about fifty percent more in taxes than the residents of Tampa. The leaders of Tampa wanted to control St. Petersburg to make sure the growth came in Tampa. In 1907 he began writing editorials demanding a separate county. He pointed out that the only way to reach the county seat in Tampa from St. Petersburg was a 160-mile trip through Lakeland and back to Tampa. Five years after he began his crusade, Pinellas County was created.

His civic campaigns left him little time to devote to the paper's financial problems. The same year Pinellas became a county, Straub was forced to sell the paper to Paul Poynter, although he stayed on as editor until his death in 1939. There is a waterfront park named for Straub, but the real tribute is the five-mile waterfront owned by the city and preserved for the public.

William Straub's St. Petersburg port

LORING CHASE WAS A SUCCESSFUL NORTHERN REALTOR WHO happened to come down with bronchitis a century ago. His illness would not go away, and someone suggested a trip to Florida might be just the thing to cure him. He made it clear he wasn't coming to Florida as a realtor, but as a vacationer. He told a friend who was urging him to consider buying land that he was "not looking for real estate, but health."

His friend persisted and eventually talked Chase into taking a carriage ride from Orlando to an area nearby. Chase was impressed. The land was beautiful and, except for some squatter cottages, nearly deserted. But he stuck with his plan not to buy land and arranged to take a steamer back to Jacksonville.

Before he could leave, his friend Oliver Chapman, a railroad owner, showed up. The two began talking and developed a plan to build an entire city. So for $13,000 the two purchased six hundred acres around lakes Osceola, Virginia, Killarney, and Maitland, and named their new land Winter Park. They laid out ambitious plans. First came a railroad depot, then a small hotel. They were so successful that Henry Sanford, the founder of Sanford, complained that Winter Park was diverting settlers from his town.

Winter Park boomed. Within a few years there were more than a score of businesses and sixty-three new homes in town. Chase lobbied the Florida Congregational Association to put its new college in Winter Park. In 1885, the FCA selected Winter Park for the site of Rollins College.

Grand hotels were built and the town competed with Palm Beach as a vacation spot for wealthy Northerners. The town drew some of the nation's most successful men, including George Pullman, George Westinghouse, and Presidents Chester Arthur and Grover Cleveland.

USUALLY, ONCE A CITY GETS A NAME, THE NAME STICKS. BUT in Florida, names have come and gone, sometimes changing two or three times. City names have been chosen for just about every possible reason. Orlando was once known as Jernigan, named for Aaron Jernigan, an early settler. Sanford was once named Mellonville after Fort Mellon. When Henry Sanford bought twelve thousand acres in the area in 1871 he also got the right to name the town anything he wanted.

Casselberry was once called Fern Park. In the 1940s, the area was developed by Hibbard Casselberry and later named for him. Fern Park is next door. Carol City in Dade County was supposed to be called Coral City, but nearby Coral Gables threatened to file suit because the name was too similar. The promoters of Coral City had already printed signs at great expense. To avoid having to make new signs, they switched the "a" and "o" and came up with Carol City.

The founders of Ormond Beach came from New Britain, Connecticut, and that's the name they gave to their new town. Later, it was changed to Ormond Beach for an early resident. Palatka was once called Buena Vista.

In the 1880s, prospector Edmund Dunne was lost in the Arizona desert. He prayed that if he survived he would one day pay homage to a saint. When he settled in Clear Lake in Pasco County, he became prominent enough to change the name to San Antonio, his patron saint.

Near St. Petersburg, Sunset Beach became Sunshine Beach. Winter Garden was Beulah, and Winter Park has had several names including Lakeview and Osceola. In south Florida there was once a town called Waldron's Homestead. The biggest employer was James Hendry. A young woman named Arcadia Albritton baked him a cake for his birthday. As a way of saying thank you, he changed the name of the town to Arcadia.

174   James Ormond Found that He Could Go Home Again

JAMES ORMOND SPENT A LIFETIME ON THE MOVE, BUT FINALLY settled in the state where he started. In 1824, eight-year-old James arrived in Florida from his native Scotland and settled on his father's plantation in what is now Volusia County. Six years later, Ormond's father died. The plantation was soon abandoned. Ormond went to Charleston, South Carolina, where he went to school for a short time, then started work in a store.

He came back to Florida to fight in the Seminole War. His unit fought with little distinction and was best remembered for one of the worst retreats in military history. During the retreat, Ormond was shot four times. He went back to Charleston to recover, then returned to Florida and became a merchant, collecting a commission on goods he bought and sold.

For about four years the business did well, then failed when a storm destroyed his stock. It was time to move on. Using some of the boards from his wrecked business, Ormond built a raft and floated up the St. Marks River until he came upon an attractive area. Along with some other people, Ormond founded the community of Newport. He began a new business and prospered.

In 1856, he moved to Atlanta and became wealthy. During the Civil War, Ormond made even more money, buying from farmers and selling to desperate city residents and the Confederate army, which he eventually joined. After the war, Ormond and his family lived in Canada, then spent several years in England before returning to Atlanta. Finally, in 1876, Ormond returned to Florida and settled near what had been his family's plantation.

In 1880, the residents of the small community where Ormond lived formed a town. They decided to name the town in his honor. Eight years later, the Ormond Beach Hotel opened; Ormond was one of the speakers at the dedication. The hotel turned the town in a major tourist center.

175 The Price Was Too High, So Flagler Moved South

IN THE 1870s, TOURISTS COULD TAKE THE STEAMBOATS TO Lake Harney in Seminole County, then travel by mule train to a place known as Sand Point. It was an area that appeared to be developing into one of the state's best resorts. Visitors stayed in the hotel of H. T. Titus, who was a Confederate blockade runner during the Civil War and also fought in Nicaragua and Cuba with revolutionaries.

Titus had become wealthy and his hotel was a special attraction, drawing tourists with its pleasant location and great seafood. As the area became associated with Titus, the name of the community became Titusville.

Meanwhile, in St. Augustine, the wealthy oilman Henry Flagler was developing that city as a tourist attraction for the wealthy. He built the massive Ponce de Leon Hotel and his wealthy friends came in droves. In the mid-1890s, a freeze swept through the state killing crops and convincing Flagler that a location a little farther south might be better.

Flagler found Titusville, or Sand Point as some still called it. He thought it would make a perfect city for the wealthy—he could build a hotel and the rich would build homes. Flagler did not figure on Louis Coleman, a resident of Titusville, who owned a large tract of land in the area. The land wasn't worth much, but once Coleman found out that Flagler—one of the richest men in the world—was interested, he quickly raised his price. He raised it so much that Flagler gave up. He abandoned his idea of turning Titusville into the nation's leading resort and went farther south. He ended up in a village on Lake Worth and there built Palm Beach.

Profits from the Civil War
Built a Florida Fortune

HENRY PLANT WAS ONE OF THE FEW PEOPLE IN THE Confederacy to grow rich during the Civil War. The money he made helped to transform Florida into a tourist mecca. Plant was the southern agent for Boston-based Adams Express Company when the war began. The company, which transported goods, was worried that its operations might be taken over by the Confederate government and decided to create a new company with only Southern stockholders. The owners selected Plant to run the company.

When the war ended, Plant had plenty of money. He began buying railroads in Georgia, then in Florida, including a three-fifths interest in the line running between Sanford and Kissimmee. He managed to do what everyone said was impossible—build a railroad between Kissimmee and Tampa in seven months.

The railroad led to a population boom in Tampa. To attract tourists, Plant built a magnificent hotel in Tampa, and he built hotels along his train route including the Hotel Kissimmee in Kissimmee and the Seminole Hotel in Winter Park. Tourists produced a tidy income for Plant, but his real money came in hauling fruit and vegetables to the North. His railroad was so efficient, he was able to greatly expand the state's orange distribution, creating a national market.

In the Spanish-American War in 1898, Plant's agents persuaded the U.S. government to establish a headquarters in Tampa. It was a financial bonanza for Tampa. Every bullet and every soldier had to be shipped through Tampa on a Plant railroad. The publicity drew even more tourists and permanent residents.

By the time of his death in 1899, Plant controlled the largest rail system in Florida and was worth more than $10 million. The railroad was absorbed by the Atlantic Coast Line and the hotels were later sold by Plant's estate. Among his namesakes is Plant City in Hillsborough County.

Plant's magnificent Tampa hotel

Unable to Join the Club, He Built His Own Resort

MOST PEOPLE DID NOT LIKE CLARENCE GEIST. HE WAS rude, arrogant, and usually crude, but he merits a small mention in Florida history. Geist started life as the son of a poor farmer in the Midwest, but he was ambitious and began to invest small amounts in utility companies. Eventually, he came to control several large water utilities in cities such as Philadelphia and Indianapolis.

In the 1920s he bought a home in exclusive Palm Beach. His money could buy a home but not membership in the exclusive Everglades Club, where the members were mostly well-bred millionaires and where Geist was most unwelcome. So, Geist decided to start his own club in Boca Raton. He purchased the Boca Raton Hotel and Club—which had gone broke during the Florida land bust—and began rounding up millionaire members. The initiation fee was a stiff $5,000 a year and the dues were extra.

Members got to use the club, but they also had to put up with Geist. For example, in the days before golf carts, golfers walked around the course. Geist did not like walking, so he had his limousine follow him around the course. It did not do much for the condition of the fairways, but it made Geist happy. In the evening, the club showed movies, but the movies could not start until Geist arrived. When he did show up, he sometimes was wearing only his bathrobe.

He ran the town of Boca Raton, population six hundred, like a dictator. His club operated only during the winter months when the wealthy flocked to Florida. He had city elections moved from November to February so his employees could vote and control the town council.

Despite his excesses, the club was popular. After he died in 1936, the club declined without Geist's money to prop it up. It has passed through several owners and today caters not to just the wealthy but to all classes.

Geist ran the Boca Raton Hotel and Club.

MARIAN NEWHALL HOROWITZ O'BRIEN, DAUGHTER OF A wealthy Philadelphia railroad executive, arrived in Florida in 1916 to pursue her dream. She was going to turn a tiny town into a city. The town, on the southern shore of Lake Okeechobee, would soon become the Chicago of the South, one booster predicted. It did not.

The town was Moore Haven, started by Seattle developer James A. Moore, who had bought 100,000 acres and started laying out streets. Moore spent money faster than it came in and by 1916 was forced to sell out. One of the purchasers was George Horowitz who moved to the community with his wife Marion, joining four hundred other hardy souls.

George Horowitz died suddenly, leaving a large hunk of the community to his widow. The rest was owned by his partner, John O'Brien. Marian and O'Brien fell in love and married, thus combining their land interests.

She was the first mayor of Moore Haven when it was incorporated in 1917. World War I pushed up the value of the town's vegetables and the future looked promising. But the natives resented the outsiders and their money. Shots were fired into the O'Brien home and one bullet grazed Marian's head.

An explosion caused by a gasoline fire destroyed much of downtown, and in 1922 floods came. The residents of Moore Haven soon learned that their town had been built in the middle of a flood zone. For about seven years, the weather had been unusually dry, and there had been no floods. When the weather returned to normal, the town found itself underwater. Finally, the O'Briens decided to move down the road twenty miles and start a new town. They named it Clewiston, after one of their investors, Tampa banker A. C. Clewis.

There was more violence, and eventually Marian and her husband gave up and moved to Detroit. In 1926, Moore Haven was nearly destroyed by a hurricane that killed two hundred residents. Clewiston went on to become the center of the Florida sugar industry. Marian died in 1931.

179   For Sanford, Labor Woes Were a Constant Problem

WHEN THE FLORIDA CITRUS INDUSTRY STARTED IN SANFORD more than a century ago, finding laborers was a problem. Henry Sanford, the father of the modern citrus industry, hired white residents, but dismissed them for failing to do the work correctly. Next, Sanford employed black workers, who did good work, but who were soon threatened by the fired white workers. At one point, the whites attacked the blacks and the black workers left town.

Henry Sanford decided to try foreign labor. He hired twenty-five Swedish workers and brought them to Florida. The Swedes were to work for Sanford in exchange for their transportation from Europe, room and board, and a small salary. The Swedes—twenty-one men and four woman—began arriving in 1871.

Almost from the start there were problems. Florida's climate was radically different from Sweden's, and the Swedes were used to working inside. There was not enough work for some of the immigrants, especially the women. Some of the workers attempted to flee to Jacksonville. Three Swedes did make their escape, but were returned.

A second group of Swedes arrived in 1872, and caused even more problems. It was difficult to get them to work, even with encouragements such as extra food. They informed their bosses that in Sweden, Christmas was a three-day holiday and they expected to have the same holiday in the United States.

When their contracts expired, those who had worked received five-acre tracts near Sanford. Henry Sanford gave up on immigrant labor and again hired blacks. And again there was violence as whites tried to force blacks from the groves. But eventually the attacks subsided. As for the Swedes who remained in the area, they founded a town three miles west of Sanford and named it New Upsala.

180   A Sewing Machine Heir Built a Legendary Resort

IN 1918 A CURIOUS PARTNERSHIP WAS FORMED BY TWO men in Palm Beach. Both were in frail health and had come to the budding resort city to die. Addison Mizner had drifted through a series of careers. Paris Singer was heir to the Singer sewing machine fortune.

Both men considered themselves amateur architects. As they talked about architecture, they began to sketch homes and lay plans to build them. With Singer supplying the money, and Mizner overseeing construction, they started building Spanish-style homes, clubs, hotels, and offices. Their timing was perfect. Palm Beach was caught in the middle of the Florida land boom.

As Mizner got into the Palm Beach project, he became more ambitious and dreamed of building a city. With the backing of T. Coleman du Pont, a member of the wealthy du Pont family, he planned Boca Raton. Mizner began selling lots, but du Pont was critical of the high-pressure advertising and complained. When the advertising continued, he complained publicly and sales stopped. All of Mizner's money was invested in the project and he went bankrupt. Boca Raton was built, but it was not what Mizner had envisioned.

Most of Palm Beach's shopping district is a result of Mizner's work, as are the town's most beautiful homes. Singer left behind his own island near Palm Beach. Today, Singer Island is being developed with exclusive homes.

FOOTNOTES TO FLORIDA HISTORY

The Duchess Took a Flyer, but Happiness Had to Wait

THERE WAS NOTHING SPECIAL ABOUT THE WOMAN WHO arrived in Pensacola in 1916. She had taken the train from Baltimore to Jacksonville, then changed for the final leg to Pensacola. She was twenty-one years old and planned to stay with a childhood friend, whose husband was in the Navy.

After she had been in Pensacola for a month, her hostess asked her to a luncheon with three young airmen. The three arrived and the young woman was immediately impressed with Earl Spencer. He asked her for a date and she accepted.

There was a whirlwind courtship. She was impressed with his job as a pilot in the earliest days of aviation—he was issued pilot license No. 11 by the Navy. Soon they were talking about a wedding. It turned out to be a splendid affair in her native Baltimore on November 8, 1916, just six months after their first meeting.

The prince and Wallis in Florida

While they were being married, a violent hurricane struck Pensacola, and when they returned to Florida to set up house, the young couple found a devastated city.

Almost from the start, the marriage went sour. He drank heavily and she hated it. So she spent a lot of her time at the movies, going nearly every day, sometimes seeing the same movie over and over again.

She did not care much for the port city of Pensacola. In 1917 the United States entered World War I. Because of his heavy drinking, her husband was not allowed to go to Europe to fly. Instead he was transferred to Boston to train pilots. She left Florida after thirteen months. The marriage ended in divorce as did her second marriage. Her third marriage lasted and became the most famous marriage of the century. The woman was Wallis Warfield Spencer Simpson, who became the Duchess of Windsor and whose third husband gave up the throne of England to marry her.

182 Warm Weather Attracted Edison to Ft. Myers

BEGINNING IN THE 1880S, FLORIDA BECAME A MECCA FOR the wealthy. Henry Flagler invited his rich friends to St. Augustine and later developed Palm Beach, a winter playground for anyone with a million dollars or more. Some of the richest Americans chose obscure Florida towns to build winter homes. John Rockefeller built a mansion in Ormond Beach.

Thomas Edison chose one of Florida's most obscure and remote cities, Ft. Myers. Edison first came to Fort Myers in the 1880s when it was little more than a village. In 1885, Edison had fallen seriously ill. His family convinced him that a rest in a warmer climate was needed. Edison agreed to go to Ft. Myers. Two days after arriving, he purchased thirteen acres on the Caloosahatchee River and ordered lumber to build a home and a laboratory.

Edison immediately became the town's most famous resident. The competition was not very tough as there were just 349 people in Fort

Thomas Edison in front of his home

Myers. When Edison offered to provide free electric lights for the town's streets, the residents declined, saying the light might bother the numerous cows that wandered the streets.

Edison's first wife died suddenly in 1884. Soon after that he met and fell in love with the daughter of a wealthy Ohio businessman. She was half his age, but the couple married and headed for Ft.

Myers for an extended honeymoon.

Edison, who had been addicted to work, soon began to ignore his business. His secretary said, "We have written him; we have telegraphed him. We get no response. He ignores the telegraph and despises the mail."

Until his death in 1931, Edison spent much of his time in Ft. Myers. A number of his friends, including President Herbert Hoover and Henry Ford, came by to visit. Ford liked the town so much he built a house near Edison's. Their fame helped transform Ft. Myers from a sleepy village into a city.

183 Walks on the Beach Led Him to Find a Fortune

AFTER WORLD WAR II, KIP WAGNER MOVED FROM OHIO TO south Brevard County. Wagner had been a building contractor in Ohio and wanted to build a motel on the Florida coast.

He liked to walk along the beach between the small community of Wabasso and Sebastian Inlet. As he walked, he found silver and gold coins in the sand. He began to ask about the coins. Others reported finding the coins, but no one had any idea where they came from.

Wagner took the coins to a friend who helped him clean them. The cleaning revealed long-hidden dates, none later than 1715. Wagner's next step was to visit the Library of Congress. Looking through old records, he found a record of a shipwreck off the Brevard coast in 1715.

He obtained more information from Spain. He learned that a group of Spanish ships laden with treasure had run into a hurricane near Cape Canaveral in 1715. The ships sank, killing more than seven hundred men, women, and children. Some of the treasure was salvaged, but the rest sank with the ships and was soon forgotten.

Wagner organized a company to search for the shipwrecks. His company arranged for salvage rights, and he acquired a $15 metal detector. The metal detector quickly led him to part of the treasure that was on the beach. He found coins, ingots, jewelry, and artifacts.

At first he was puzzled by the large black rocks he found buried with the treasure. A cleaning showed that the "rocks" were actually huge clumps of gold coins turned black. The clumps contained as many as fifteen hundred gold coins.

He pushed on with his effort, this time diving in the ocean. By 1966, Wagner had found more than $3.5 million in gold and other valuables. Wagner died in 1972, but the search for the treasure continues.

PROTECTING THE MANATEE HAS BECOME A MAJOR ISSUE IN Florida during the past twenty years, but interest in the manatee goes back hundreds of years. There is evidence that the manatee may have been the source for stories about mermaids. Sailors returning from voyages to North America talked of seeing the manatees, and with every telling the story changed until the creatures became attractive mermaids.

In 1760, the British government discussed the fate of the manatee. The Lords of His Majesty's Right Honorable Privy Council for Plantation Affairs named a new governor for East Florida and gave him instructions about his new job. The council chose James Grant and went over the usual list of concerns about East Florida including problems with Indians, finances, and defense.

There was another issue that came under the heading, "Additional Instruction." The King of England learned that "several Parts of the coast . . . near the point called the Cape of Florida are frequented and resorted to by the animals called Manatee, or the Sea Cow." The King was concerned about protecting the manatees from fast-moving ships or from pirates.

The interest was economic. The British crown was intrigued with the "quality of oil they produce" and thought "great profit" could be "made by persons carrying on this species of fishing." The new governor was ordered not to sell or give any coastal land near water "frequented by these animals, where they have their Colonies or landing places." The manatee already faced a threat from the Indians, who used the creature as a source of food.

The number of manatees declined until 1890, when Martin Heade launched a campaign to save the manatee. In a sarcastic letter to *Field and Stream* in 1896, Heade wrote, "Florida has legislators of wonderful foresight, who can always be relied on to see the danger of exterminating game and plumage birds after they have disappeared, and it's hardly worthwhile to trouble ourselves about the rapidly disappearing manatee, for our wise salons (legislators) will attend to that." Heade's movement gained support and the manatee was saved from extinction.

185 Foster Wrote the State Song Without Seeing Florida

NO ONE KNOWS WHY STEPHEN FOSTER DECIDED TO NAME his song, "Way Down Upon the Swanee River"—more popularly known as "Old Folks at Home." When he wrote the song in Pittsburgh in 1851, he had never seen the Suwannee River, and there is no evidence that he was ever in Florida. Foster once lived in South Carolina and the song was originally named for one of that state's rivers, "Way Down Upon the Pee Dee River."

In 1935 the Florida Legislature adopted "Old Folks" as the official state song replacing "Florida, My Florida." Foster changed both the spelling and the pronunciation of the river to fit his song. The river is supposed to be pronounced "Sue-wannee," but Foster pronounced and spelled it "Swanee."

Today, the song is considered offensive, although a few word changes over the years have made it more palatable for official state functions. The song was written by Foster in dialect and paints a bucolic picture of plantation life in the days of slavery: "Still longing for de old plantation, And for de old folks at home."

Although Foster's chorus contains the line, "Oh, darkies, how my heart grows weary," when the new Florida Capitol building was dedicated in 1978, the line was changed in the official program to read, "Oh, brothers, how my heart grows weary."

186 Pilgrims Get the Credit, but the Spanish Had the Idea

THANKSGIVING HAS BECOME AN AMERICAN TRADITION AS millions of Americans envision the Pilgrims sitting down with the Indians to enjoy a celebration. But Florida historians argue that it was not the Pilgrims who held the first Thanksgiving in the New World.

As every schoolchild learns, after the Pilgrims landed at Plymouth Rock they sat down with the Indians and had Thanksgiving dinner. What they really had was a harvest festival, a traditional event to mark a successful harvest. The festival lasted three days. However, employers throughout the country have chosen to ignore the fact that the original celebrants got three days off, not one. The Pilgrims actually held their first Thanksgiving two years later in 1623 to celebrate the end of a drought.

But perhaps children in school plays should be dressing like Spanish soldiers, not Pilgrims. Dr. Michael Gannon, one of Florida's leading historians, says the first Thanksgiving was celebrated in Florida nearly a century before the Pilgrims.

Gannon says the Spanish held a thanksgiving celebration every time they landed in Florida. The first was at Tampa Bay in 1529. Another thanksgiving was celebrated in 1559 in Pensacola and a third in St. Augustine on September 8, 1565, when the Spanish shared their meal with the Timucua Indians.

There is no record of what was served in St. Augustine, but Gannon believes it was probably salted pork and garbanzo beans. Why has the Spanish thanksgiving been overlooked? "Because it's the victors who write the histories," Gannon said. "The British established the traditions and holidays."

187 It Was a Special Delivery to Send a Letter in 1880s

IN THE EARLY 1880S, IF YOU LIVED IN THE SMALL VILLAGE OF Miami and sent a letter to Jupiter—ninety miles north—you waited a long time for your reply. The letter went by ship from Miami to Key West, then to Cuba. From Havana it made its way to New York by steamer, then back to Florida by train and yet another boat.

The letter and its reply each took six weeks. Miamians complained to the federal government, and a mailman was hired to deliver the mail between Miami and Jupiter. But hiring a mailman did not solve the problem. There was no road between Miami and Jupiter. Anyone delivering the mail had to walk on the beach, a difficult walk through the sand dunes.

It turned out that the only place to walk easily was where the sand was hard—where the surf came ashore. Still, the route took several days, and walking in the surf meant the mailman's shoes got wet. So, the mailman took them off, and the legend of "The Barefoot Mailman" was born.

The route existed for nearly ten years. The mailman was paid $300 per year to begin with, but the salary was later doubled. In 1887 a railroad opened to serve part of the route, although the mailman still had to walk from Palm City—now Palm Beach—to Miami. As the mailman walked his route, he would stop to fish and pick wild fruit.

The work could be dangerous, and one mailman lost his life while swimming across a flooded stream. The barefoot mailman was forgotten until the 1930s when Theodore Pratt wrote a book, which was turned into the movie, *The Barefoot Mailman.*

188   State Flags Rose and Fell as Rulers Came and Went

IT STARTED IN 1513, WHEN THE FLAG OF THE SPANISH KING was raised, and it continued until 1966, when the Legislature changed the state flag for the final time (at least so far). In the 453 years in between, more flags have flown over Florida than any other state—so many, in fact, that no one knows the exact number. At least seventeen state and national flags—including French, Spanish, British, and American—have flown over all or part of Florida.

From 1799 to 1817 there were a number of attempts to overthrow the Spanish. Three unsuccessful attempts to overthrow the Spanish started on Amelia Island, each with a flag in readiness. And when West Florida declared its independence from Spain in 1810, it had its own flag for ten weeks.

State flags have been a particular problem for Florida. The first state flag featured blue, orange, red, white, and green stripes with a small American flag in the lefthand corner. The words "Let us alone" were written across the orange stripe.

During the Civil War, there was a flag designed by "The Ladies of Broward's Nick" with three large stars, a blue circle, seven stripes, and the words: "The rights of the South at all hazards."

After the Civil War, the state adopted its dullest flag, the state seal set in a field of white. When it hung limp, it was impossible to see the state seal and it looked like a white sheet. The Legislature added two diagonal red stripes in 1900 and changed the shape from square to rectangular in 1966.

189   For a Millionaire, Changing the Divorce Law Was Simple

HENRY FLAGLER HAD A PROBLEM. HE WAS ONE OF THE RICHest men in the world, a partner of John D. Rockefeller in Standard Oil and the developer of the east coast of Florida from St. Augustine to Palm Beach. His problem was his second wife. Flagler's first wife had died in 1881 with her faithful husband and her nurse, Alice Shourds, by her side.

Shourds, who was thirty-five, had tried unsuccessfully to be an actress before turning to nursing, but she eventually found an even more lucrative career: second wife of Henry Flagler. The two were married soon after his first wife's death, but soon the new wife started doing unusual things.

She used coffee cream on her skin, burnt cork on her eyebrows, and red dye on her cheeks instead of standard makeup. She became convinced that the czar of Russia was madly in love with her and was on his way to take her away.

She thought the Flagler mansion was full of Russian spies. At social engagements, she frequently threw fits of temper. Finally her husband had her committed to a mental institution, and in 1899 she was ruled incurably insane.

Flagler was upset about his wife—but not so upset that he overlooked thirty-four-year-old Mary Lily Kenan. Flagler, who was seventy-one by that time, began dating her, and when people began to talk, Mary insisted they marry.

Flagler could not legally divorce his wife on grounds of insanity. So he decided to have Florida's divorce law changed. No one is sure how much money he spent to influence the legislature, but talk was that Flagler Hall at Stetson University in DeLand was built with a donation designed to influence passage of the bill. The legislature passed a law allowing those with insane spouses to obtain a divorce. There was an outpouring of anger, but Flagler ignored it and soon married.

Four years later the legislature reversed its action. Henry Flagler lived for another dozen years. His third wife survived him by just four years, dying at the age of fifty-one. As for Alice, she lived until 1930, spending her time in an asylum, waiting for the czar of Russia.

190 An Inventor Was on the Trail of an Air Conditioning Miracle

DR. JOHN GORRIE MIGHT HAVE GONE DOWN IN THE HISTORY books along with Thomas Edison and Alexander Graham Bell. Instead he died a penniless laughingstock. No one laughs at Gorrie's invention today. Indeed, going without it for a single day during August in Florida is almost inconceivable. John Gorrie was the first man to obtain a patent for a system of air conditioning.

Necessity was indeed the mother of invention for Dr. Gorrie, who began a medical practice in Apalachicola in 1833 and was immediately confronted with the battle against yellow fever. He felt that if he could keep his patients in a cool environment, he could help them. He put together a system that forced the air entering the room to pass over blocks of ice suspended from the ceiling. There was, of course, a problem getting ice in Florida in 1833. Gorrie began to experiment with machines to manufacture ice. Within a year he was able to produce ice and cool rooms in his small hospital.

In 1850 he received a patent for his machine. Public acceptance of his invention did not exactly take off like a rocket, and after his only financial backer died, Dr. Gorrie went broke putting his own money into promoting his invention. His debts piled up, and he took to writing under a pen name to avoid those who made fun of him and his invention. He became a recluse and died in 1855 at the age of 52.

191 Who's to Blame for Picking Such Poor County Names?

IT IS FINALLY TIME TO ADMIT IT: WHEN IT CAME TO PICKING names for counties, Florida simply did not do a good job. In fact, the people who named counties were so hard up for ideas it has two counties named for the same guy: Hernando de Soto. One county took his first name in 1843, and a second, his last name in 1887.

DeSoto County was so big, it was divided into five counties in the 1920s. One of the new counties was to be named Seminole, until it was pointed out that a Seminole County was already being formed and that it would be somewhat confusing to have two counties with the same name. In its place, they picked the name Hardee, for Governor Cary Hardee, a small-time politician defeated the next time he ran for office. DeSoto was not the only county to go through such a change. Early on, the Spanish named a fort near Cape Canaveral, Santa Lucia. Eventually it became St. Lucie County, a huge county encompassing a big chunk of east and central Florida. It got so big there was pressure to divide it up.

As it happened, Theodore Washington Brevard had been elected state comptroller two years earlier—and who better to name a county after than the state comptroller? Did Brevard ever visit the county that bears his name? Not that we know of. For half a century, Saint Lucie was off the map. Then, in 1905, part of Brevard was taken and renamed St. Lucie, the only county name to have existed twice.

And then there's the county that has never existed: Pinkney County. In 1835, the territorial legislature was in the process of creating a county and decided to name it after William Pinkney of Maryland. As they were about to vote, word arrived that a group of Indians had killed Major Francis Dade—so they named it after him instead. The problem was, a Northern mapmaker, apparently thinking that the Legislature intended for the new county to be on the spot where Dade died, placed the new county north of Tampa. The maps were corrected—and Dade was moved to south Florida.

His Strangest Script Called for Phony Buried Treasure

BEN HECHT IS BEST KNOWN AS THE WRITER OF THE HIT play and movie, *The Front Page*, and for his work on such film scripts as *Scarface* and *Gone with the Wind*. He is less well known for a giant hoax he pulled in Florida in 1925. That was the year he arrived in Miami with his fiancee to visit a friend.

Even though he made a fortune from his writing, Hecht was frequently broke, the result of high living. Florida was in the midst of a land boom, and Hecht figured there was a way he could profit. He wrangled an introduction with Charles Ort, the president of the Key Largo Corporation. The company was getting ready to sell lots on Key Largo, and Hecht thought he could help.

Hecht was invited to meet with the directors of the company. His plan to help them sell lots was actually a scam. Hecht said they could sell lots by convincing people that Key Largo was the home for Spanish treasure left by pirates. To do this, he proposed a treasure hunt. A yacht would be chartered in New York to take fifty society women and others down to Key Largo, then turn them loose to look for a treasure. Hecht and his friends would plant some treasure where the women would be sure to find it.

The directors asked how much all this would cost. Hecht said he and a partner would require $5,000 a week for twelve weeks as a minimum—an incredible sum in 1925—plus the expense of renting the yacht and other related costs. He convinced the president of Cuba to lend him some Spanish gold coins, acquired some Spanish vases, and had them buried on Key Largo.

Then trouble set in. Hecht could not find any society women to take part in his stunt. He came up with a second plan. He paid a beachcomber to help them and gave him $100 to "discover" the treasure.

Hecht sent telegrams to two hundred newspapers informing them that a half-million dollars in treasure had been found in Key Largo. The story created a sensation and land sales in Key Largo soared. Hecht was presented with a new twelve-week contract and a pay raise. But he sensed that trouble was brewing. He became convinced that the land boom was about to bust. He quit his job and urged the directors of the Key Largo company to bail out quickly. They would not listen.

Hecht was right and the boom crashed. Land that sold for thousands of dollars one day, was worthless the next. The Key Largo developers were forced to liquidate. Hecht returned to Chicago with his money. He used $10,000 to pay his estranged wife for a divorce and then remarried. As for Key Largo president Ort, he was last seen sleeping in his car in a parking lot.

193 Changing Names Became Normal for the St. Johns River

THE ST. JOHNS RIVER WAS A MYSTERY TO EARLY SAILORS FOR nearly a century. It flows north—the only U.S. river of its length to do so—and its headwaters are hidden in the swamps of Indian River County. No one knows who was the first European to discover the St. Johns, but by 1520, the river was appearing on crude maps and was called River of Currents because of its swift currents.

The Indians called it Welaka, meaning river of lakes. In 1562, the French explorer, Jean Ribault, built a fort near present-day Jacksonville and named the river Rivière de Mai, because he found it during May. His fort was wiped out by the Spanish and the name vanished.

The Spanish called it Rio de San Mateo after their fort. When the fort was abandoned, the river came to be called San Juan, after another Spanish fort. When the British took over in 1763, they changed San Juan to St. John's. When Florida became a U.S. territory, the apostrophe was dropped.

There is a story that when tourists would ask how far the river went, the natives would reply, "To hell and blazes." Which is why, in the marshlands west of Melbourne near the river's headwaters, there is a lake named Lake Helen Blazes.

194 A Fortune Built Florida's Most Magnificent Mansion

JAMES DEERING MADE HIS FORTUNE AS A FOUNDER OF International Harvester. Building tractors made him rich, but he longed to build a palatial mansion. First, he needed to find the perfect spot to build. He traveled to Egypt, North Africa, and the French Riviera but failed to find the perfect spot. In 1912, he visited his friend, William Jennings Bryan, in Miami and fell in love with the area. He purchased 130 acres on Biscayne Bay for a mere $25,000.

Clearing the land took four months as the workmen tried not to disturb

Villa Vizcaya, Deering's Miami mansion

the trees. To build the main house, Deering hired more than one thousand workers. They built a stucco wall around the property, then began the main house.

The seventy-six-room mansion called for the finest materials, and artisans were brought from Europe to make the cabinets, cut the stones, paint, and plant beautiful gardens. Deering leased a nearby warehouse where he built sample rooms to test materials and designs. Deering supervised every detail. If a room or hallway did not please him, he ordered it torn out and rebuilt to new specifications.

Four years after he started, Deering moved into the house. The total cost was nearly $20 million. For his money Deering built one of the most magnificent homes in the world. To maintain the house, he employed four butlers, four housemen, six maids, gardeners, and two chefs.

He then turned his attention to furnishing his house and making the gardens a world-famous showplace. He gathered furniture from throughout the world, including chairs from the Combe Abbey in England. Deering died in 1925, and his house passed to his nieces. In 1952 they turned it over to Dade County for use as an art gallery.

195 Vacationing in 1800s Kissimmee was Hardly a Pleasure

A CENTURY AGO, A TRIP FROM SANFORD TO KISSIMMEE WAS an adventure. Indeed, in 1886, *Harper's Magazine* paid Henri Dauge to write about the journey. Here is part of what he wrote:

There were eight of us who came down on the tri-weekly 'construction train' then running from Sanford to Kissimmee City. Having reached Kissimmee City, we pitched our tents first on an island near it, at the head of the big blue lake Tohopekaliga.

The new town, with its sixteen houses, none painted or whitewashed, had at least the beginnings of civilization— a baker's, a restaurant, and hotel in process of erection.

On Friday morning the four restless spirits set forth in a sailboat. The little boat, 19 feet long and five and a half wide, went gaily before the breeze across the blue waters of Tohopekaliga. It was only at sunset that we at last wearily made the beach we had left in the morning, and there we encamped for the night. This was to be our resting place for two nights.

The party spent a week on Lake Tohopekaliga and the rivers, swamps, and streams near it, killing an alligator and hunting game.

When we danced into view of Kissimmee across the blue waves of Tohopekaliga, we heard the engine of the tri-weekly train whistle as it came in. We caught it in time for the return trip, and also had time for an excursion to the bakery. Brown, unshaven, with worn and torn raiment, and a cheerful appreciation of baker's bread, we took our places in the fresh and new passenger coach. Kissimmee City seemed to us the heart of civilization.

We had subsisted on corn bread and coffee for the most part. We did not disclose the fact that the deer's horns we had brought home were purchased from the Seminoles.

196   Championship Fight Was a Battle Royal Outside the Ring

INSIDE THE RING, IT WAS ONE OF THE DULLEST FIGHTS EVER staged, but outside it was a battle royal involving everyone from the governor to the state militia. The year was 1894, the place, Jacksonville, and "Gentleman Jim" Corbett was the heavyweight champion. His managers were looking for a place to hold a match with British champion Charley Mitchell. The Duval Athletic Club bid for the fight, and a bout was scheduled for January 25. The winning boxer was to receive $20,000.

Almost immediately protests began, and the governor ordered the fight cancelled. The mayor of Jacksonville called prizefighting "the brutal instincts of humanity." Ministers held meetings to organize opposition.

When Mitchell arrived to begin training, he was arrested under a law which outlawed prizefighting. He posted $1,500 bail and began training. The problem for police was that they could not arrest anyone until the fight actually took place.

Citizens picked sides in the dispute and soon fights were breaking out between pro-and anti-fight forces. In desperation, city officials declared martial law and sent for the state militia in Sanford to keep order. The fighters went to court, however, and secured an injunction to prevent officials from interfering with the bout.

The fight began on schedule at the site of the old fairgrounds with thousands of spectators on hand. In the second round, Corbett knocked Mitchell down once. Mitchell went down twice in the third round before Corbett finished him off with a powerful right.

As soon as the fight was over, both men were arrested on assault charges. They posted $5,000 bail and left town. Corbett was found not guilty and charges against Mitchell were dropped. For both men, the fight marked the high point in their careers. Mitchell faded into obscurity and Corbett never again won a championship fight.

197 Baseball Spring Training Found a Home in Florida

MORE THAN FIFTY YEARS AGO, BASEBALL MANAGER BRANCH Rickey signed up Jackie Robinson, the first black to play in the major leagues. But his other contribution to baseball history is also worthy of note. It was Rickey who created spring training in Florida.

Before Rickey, spring training was haphazard and held in such places as Cairo, Illinois; Hot Springs, Arkansas; and Valdosta, Georgia. The teams—usually strapped for cash—just worked out a bit before starting the season.

In 1913, Rickey, manager of the St. Louis Browns, took his team to St. Petersburg for training. The Chicago Cubs copied the idea, setting up training in neighboring Tampa. The teams played the first spring training games against each other, although the "visiting" team had to travel two hours by boat across Tampa Bay for each match.

Next to come South—in 1919—were the Boston Red Sox. The New York Yankees and the Red Sox played in Florida before four thousand fans, who saw Babe Ruth hit the longest recorded home run in baseball—579 feet. Ruth was fond of Florida and even became an honorary Tampa Boy Scout. But he claimed that an alligator lived in the northern edge of the Yankee training field and refused to go near that area.

Lou Gehrig and Babe Ruth with a Florida fan

In 1921, Joe Tinker, a Chicago Cubs player for fifteen years, founded a team in Orlando called Tinker's Tigers. Tinker had been a renowned player and had made a fortune with a land development company. The city of Orlando built Tinker Field for the former player's Tigers. Tinker then persuaded the Cincinnati Reds to hold spring training in Orlando. They were followed by the Washington Senators, who later became the Minnesota Twins.

Breaking Baseball's Color Barrier Was Tough in Florida

JACKIE ROBINSON IS BEST KNOWN AS THE FIRST BLACK TO play major league baseball. But he also may be responsible for the Dodgers moving from Daytona Beach to Vero Beach. Robinson was signed by the Brooklyn Dodgers after World War II. He was assigned to the Dodgers' Montreal farm club, far removed from the racial taunts he would have to face in the United States.

But first, he had to endure spring training in Florida. Even before Robinson arrived at the Dodgers' camp in Daytona Beach in 1947, the city manager announced that Robinson would be required to abide by all segregation laws and could not stay at local hotels.

When Robinson reported for pre-training in Sanford, citizens met with Dodger manager Branch Rickey and said blacks could not play ball on the same field with whites. Robinson went back to Daytona Beach. When he went to Jacksonville to play a game, city officials ordered it canceled. DeLand officials also canceled a Dodger game rather than allow Robinson to play.

In Sanford, Robinson was in the lineup for two innings, even getting to bat once. Then the Sanford police chief arrived and told club officials that Robinson would have to be removed from the field. Rickey became convinced he needed a spring camp where none of his players—black or white—would be bothered.

He settled on Vero Beach and a camp with plenty of room. But even in Vero Beach there were problems. A rumor spread that black pitcher Don Newcombe had attacked a white man. Rickey met with officials and threats of lynching subsided after Rickey agreed that Newcombe would not leave the camp.

The racial problems began to subside after the civil rights movement began in the late 1950s and the Major League Players Association demanded an end to discrimination against black players. There was also an economic factor to consider: teams began practicing in Arizona where there was less racial discrimination. Florida cities realized that unless they adjusted their policies, spring baseball would be nothing more than a memory.

199   Hey Cracker! Is That an Insult or Compliment?

IN 1991 THE HIGHLANDS COUNTY SCHOOL BOARD FACED A controversy over naming an elementary school. The board voted to name a new school Cracker Trail Elementary School. There were protests that the word "Cracker" was a derogatory term, and the board decided to rename the school. Then, people complained that the word "Cracker" was not an insult. The board went back to its original plan.

The term "cracker" has dozens of different meanings, some as old as Florida. The first reference to it appears in 1509. Research by James Lewis of Western Carolina University found that the word came from England, where it originally meant a braggart or a talker. In the New World, the term came to stand for a host of unpleasant characteristics. Some believe cracker was synonymous with criminals.

The word is used in a 1776 letter: "I should explain to your Lordship what is meant by Crackers; a name they have got from being great boasters; they are a lawless set of rascals on the frontiers of Virginia, Maryland, the Carolinas, and Georgia, who often change their abode."

The first reference to a cracker in Florida appears in 1790, when the Spanish governor of East Florida wrote that the crackers in Florida were wild, nomadic, and would not heed government authority.

Gradually, the term came to be applied to Florida cowboys, many of whom were like the earlier crackers. At times it has been an affectionate term, but most dictionaries say it has negative connotations, usually associated with poor whites.

200   Florida State Was a Champ Before Anyone Realized

IN 1947, FLORIDA STATE UNIVERSITY, WHICH HAD BEEN A women's college since 1905, opened its doors to men and began to organize a football program. But it wasn't the first time men had played football at the school. From 1902 to 1904, Florida State fielded a team and compiled a record of 7-6-1 according to research by Ric Kabat of Gainesville College in Georgia.

The team even had its own cheer:

> Boom-a-lacka, boom-a-lacka, bow, wow, wow!
> Ching-a-lacka, ching-a-lacka! Who are we?
> We are the boys of FSC!

But they did not have a nickname. The players wore gold uniforms with a large purple "F" on their chests.

The team played other colleges and city teams. Twice, they beat a team from Bainbridge, Georgia. Their schedule included Georgia Tech, Stetson University, East Florida Seminary, and the University of Florida. In 1903 the University of Florida was located in Lake City. Florida State won the game 12-0.

In 1904 Florida State defeated the University of Florida 35-0. In 1905, the legislature overhauled the state university system and Florida State became a college for women.

INDEX OF FLORIDA PEOPLE AND PLACES